Family Companion Dog

An Owner's Manual
for Relationship-Centered Leadership

Renea L. Dahms DipCBST, RMT, CTDI

Title: Family Companion Dog – An Owner's Manual for Relationship-Centered Leadership

Publisher: Lulu

www.lulu.com

Author: Renea L. Dahms DipCBST, RMT, CTDI

Photos: Renea L. Dahms unless otherwise noted

Cover art and book design: Renea L. Dahms and Shelly Volsche

Book layout and format: Shelly Volsche

Copy Editor: Hilary Lane

ISBN 978-1-5-105-74107-4

"If it's not fun, you're not doing it right"
— National Institute For Play

Pawsitively Unleashed! LLC
Renea L. Dahms DipCBST,CTDI,RMT
Behavior & Training Director

www.pawsitivelyunleashed.com
info@pawsitivelyunleashed.com

"A wolf would flip another wolf against his will ONLY if he were planning to kill it. Can you imagine what a forced alpha roll does to the psyche of our dogs?"
— Dr. Ian Dunbar

Leading professionals speak out for
The Family Companion Dog manual

"Renea has an excellent knowledge of animal training techniques, and conveys concepts in an easy-to-understand, and simple-to-implement style. Homework exercises reinforce new skills, and hand-hold dog and owner through the learning process. Positive training methods are fun for the dog and enhance the dog-owner relationship. You'll come out of Renea's course with not only a happily trained dog, but the skills to continue a successful relationship."
    — Kyra Sundance, world-renowned trainer and author of *101 Dog Tricks*

"This book provides easy-to-understand concepts and exercises in a way that makes sense to the average readers and their dogs. Anyone can learn from this primer, solely using reward-based training and creative ideas that use some out-of-the box ideas you won't get elsewhere.
    — Hilary Lane, owner of Fang Shui Canines Training, co-founder of the American Treibball
        Association, and certified Treibball trainer.

"Renea Dahms has a great understanding of the process needed to help dog guardians to achieve a well trained dog. Following her instructions will result in just that!"
    — Debby McCullen CDBC, author of *How Many Dogs? Using Positive Reinforcement Training to
        Manage a Multiple Dog Household*

"Delightful to see another positive-reinforcement based resource available for humans who love their dogs and want to train them using scientifically sound methods that enhance trust and relationship. Brava Renea!"
    — Pat Miller CBCC-KA, CPDT-KA, trainer and author of *The Power of Positive Dog Training*

What families really need are positive, gentle training techniques combined with scientifically valid information—and that is exactly what Renea's manual delivers. Owners will learn simple but important exercises to help their dogs master new skills, and will come away with an understanding of how to apply these important behavior concepts to any situation that might arise. A valuable read for any dog-loving family!
    — Nicole Wilde, Author *Don't Leave Me!* and *Help for Your Fearful Dog*

Renea has created a fun and easy to follow guide for families through the Family Companion Dog. Sharing her personal experience and story offers an immediate connection between she and the reader. As a dog behavior consultant I loved that she offers multiple ways to go about training similar behaviors. Readers will definitely find ways to succeed with their dog in a fun and bonding way. Building and strengthening our bonds with our family dogs is so rewarding and this book is an excellent tool that will speak to many families!
    — Jennifer Shryock, Founder of Family Paws Parent Education, Creator of Dogs & Storks and
        Dog and Baby Connection

Dedication

This book is dedicated to my Uncle Joe, who encouraged me to write and do great things. His constant praise of my "prolific" writing skills throughout my childhood has stuck with me, and while I never did become an English teacher, write I did. May you rest in peace knowing better late than never.

And to my mom (Diane Spare), my sister (Amy Lupercio) and my aunt (Jane Jones) thank you for believing in me and knowing one day I would do good things.

I would also like to thank my husband, Bruce, for all his support of my crazy dog stuff, which took over his otherwise quiet life.

And of course to my dogs, whom without I would not be the trainer and behavior person I am today. They are truly the spirit that leads me.

I cannot ever begin to thank Hilary Lane or Shelly Volsche enough for reading through, editing, formatting, cheerleading and making this more enjoyable to accomplish.

How to use this book

This book was designed as a workbook. Each chapter represents a week of training. In a class setting, the learning concepts would be introduced and the training exercises practiced; students would then spend the week between classes working on the exercises.

Each chapter ends with a training log that already has the exercises (for that chapter) listed for you, as well as a space for any training notes. I recommend that you train each skill (exercise) with a set number of treats (10, for example) and only use a treat for a successful attempt. After making that number of attempts, mark how many were successful on the log. For example, your dog made 8 successful attempts at sit on verbal cue, you would write 8 in the space next to that behavior for that session. This allows you to see if your dog is making progress and how reliable he is getting at the behaviors.

This book can also be used by training professionals, as it outlines a total 7-week training class in basic manners that are considered important for companion animals.

I highly recommend you read through the entire book before beginning the training exercises, as there is a lot of valuable information contained throughout.

Enjoy working with your dog; do not be afraid to write in your book or mark up your training logs. For those who find books a treasured item (such as I do), I have also put the training logs at the back of the book so you can easily copy them without marking up your book. But really, it is a workbook, so mark away!

Connecting with your dog

Before beginning a training session (or competition) it is always good to connect with your dog. A really good method for this is "mat work" (bodywork). You can use TTouch© techniques (Linda Tellington-Jones), basic massage, Reiki or any other hands on method you are familiar and comfortable with. My dogs happen to love Reiki and suck it up like sponges; they also enjoy a good massage. There are several good books available on these topics.

Take several minutes to work with your dog in a quiet, calm location (as best you can based on your environment) to offer the technique of your choice. This is a good way to calm an anxious, or high drive dog, it also can become part of reframing (reframing is about changing your dog's emotional state toward a situation, circumstance and so on. It is way of showing him things can be associated in a new way that is more desirable.) a situation by adding a new "routine" to your activity.

Remember…

Training is a lifelong journey for both you and your dog. Take the time to do it right. Take the time to build a relationship that allows you to be the leader you want to be, and more importantly the one your dog respects you for.

Enjoy….

Forward…

I've reviewed plenty of books over the years and I have always been able to hold onto my own objectivity. I found myself engaged this time, in each word, each sentence, each thought. I played out the recipes in my mind as though the words had come to life on a canvas. This project was a life changer for the author who I have come to respect for the painstaking work, effort and time encased within the pages I read. It became apparent that she had put a lot of thought into her work so that it may resonate with her readers and the dogs they so cherish.

It was no easy task to write a forward for a colleague of mine as I consider this an immense honour and privilege. Keeping with the author's theme of 'different' and refreshing, I took a bit of a different route in putting this together. While reviewing the book I happened across some well said passages and thought I would include them in this note. I'm convinced that the readers will enjoy the same experience I have and so much more.

…"Your job is to find those reinforcers your dog will happily work for. Reinforcement has gotten a bad rap as being all about cookie training, which is simply not true, it is about finding what is reinforcing enough to your dog to make him want to work for it." Renea Dahms

This passage sets the perspective and mood right from the get go! Renea has had the forethought to reach the dog enthusiast who can simultaneously catch their favorite TV show and teach their dog an exercise. I love the idea of competing for couch space when training the family dog! I found myself smiling and nodding in appreciation as the author flirted with time. She rhymes off easy and simple approaches to modern dog training using real world examples that have a wide range of appeal for those entering into the task of relationship building with their dog. One of the challenges every good dog trainer faces today is the time. I love Renea's fabulous approach, like the old adage, if you can't beat 'em, you may as well join them! Welcome to the new norm of today's pet guardian. I found yet another wonderful opportunity to quote Renea that eloquently frames the author's perspective on the methodology of dog training in today's society, from beginning to end.

"It is my personal belief that when training your dog you should train him to perfection… When we are in the training process we work hard and have expectations, when we slow down or stop training we get lax and slack off. If you train your dog to the level you can live with, your dog will get sloppy and revert back to where you started. If you train to perfection, your dog will get sloppy and end up with what you can live with." Renea Dahms

This just sums it all up for me and I'm confident the reader will agree! Imagine teaching an exercise that requires your dog to walk forward with you in a way that doesn't pull your arm socket out of place, and to top it off, begin the exercise walking backwards! I happen to have adopted a new dog to my household. While reading the book I was intrigued and motivated to get out and try this different approach to teaching your dog to walk nicely on a leash. I have to report that it works!

"Have a plan when working with your dog. Know what you want to accomplish and how you will get there. Describe the behavior you want, do not simply say "I want my dog to lie down". What is involved? What does it look like? How does he get there? When you do this you are better able to reinforce any small steps to the behavior if need be…" Renea Dahms

The knowledge Renea has shared with her readers definitely will take the 'I don't get it or it doesn't work' out of the process! Renea offers an insightful definition of the process, and adds a sample goal setting plan at the end of the book! It's not every day that I have read a 'how to' manual on the topic of dog training that includes the need to set proper goals.

A must read. The book helps the students of dog training through the process of relationship building. It is a testament to the author's profound desire to ensure that her students have every possible tool to reach success! From reliable recalls for the dog park, to couch exercises, and teaching your dog to walk nice on a leash by first walking backwards were just some of the examples that I found useful and different! These are the exercises and approach that the modern dog guardian needs to learn to set their dog up for success in today's society.

Lastly, the tribute to dog bite prevention was a real treat for me. As the co-creator of the world's premier dog bite prevention organization, I couldn't be more pleased with Renea's dedication to remind her readers about this most important topic.

Teresa Lewin
www.nobiteme.com
www.doggonesafe.com

Table of Contents

Acknowledgement

This book is the culmination of years of working with dogs; from my own pack to those of my training class participants, and private training and grooming clients.

Every dog that has entered my life has offered me an invaluable learning experience and a new piece of knowledge about working with dogs on their own individual levels. I am forever blessed for having known and loved them, trained them, taught their owners how to work with them or to have just given them a strong foundation before going to their "forever homes".

The purpose of this book is to help the average dog owner learn how to better understand their dog, to remind the avid competitor / trainer why they started this adventure in the first place, and offer the training instructor a curriculum or possibly different prospective from puppy classes through competition oriented training. It is based on the exact exercises used in my classes, as they are taught. Each chapter contains learning concepts and exercises to do week by week. The end of the book contains "Training Tips" for a quick reference.

I recommend you first read the book in its entirety, then proceed with the training exercises. Each chapter contains valuable learning concepts that will aid you in your journey.

I hope you enjoy reading it as much as I enjoyed writing it and that you find as much use in its contents as I found in researching the solutions to all my dog training woes.

Renea

Building the Bonds That Last

When was the last time you looked your dog square in the eye? Do you remember why you started training, competing or just owning dogs? Every good trainer/handler has a timeless bond with their training companion. They dance to the beat of the same drum and are a well oiled machine — a team.

It is my heartfelt belief that one should look at their dog as a partner and develop a relationship and bond based not on power and domination, but of compassion and partnership. You will find your dog a far more willing partner when not spending so much time dominating him.

For my 18th birthday, I purchased "Lady," a wonderful Dalmatian puppy. She was the light of my life and constant companion until she passed away just shy of her 11th birthday. She hung out with me all the time. She was a favorite at the park, loved her McDonald's plain hamburger no bun on our drives home from college, and was the mascot of my [now ex-]husband's college apartment complex. Lady and I had a terrific bond and she was one of those fantastic dogs that were just wonderfully "trained" by our very time together.

Every night I would take Lady on an hour or longer walk through our small Central Wisconsin town totally off-lead and never worried she would do anything but walk with me. At our apartment complex (after college) she could be let out through our patio door and would sit for hours in the grass just off the patio slab; she never barked at anyone passing by and was just a marvel. All this was done by respect, treats, praise and just plain old showing her what I liked. I had never taken a formal "obedience class" and knew nothing of the aversive training methods of the choke and strangle crowd.

I took my first "formal dog training class" in 1995 with Sable, my young black lab. Having grown up with well-mannered dogs, I was excited to take an actual class. I showed up with my dog, on a regular collar, with a zip-lock baggie full of tasty dog treats, excited to learn and have fun with my dog.

The first thing the instructor told me was to get rid of the treats, and the buckle collar as I needed to have a choke collar and treats were "evil." I really did not understand how treats could be bad when we had used them for every dog we had when I was a child and my then 8-year-old Dalmatian who never left the yard, walked all over town with no leash, never barked, came when called and the list goes on, but I did as I was told and my introduction to traditional correction-based-training was born.

I learned how to "teach" a sit with a quick upward jerk of the choke chain, releasing upon the sit and a quick jerk forward as I begin moving to "teach" the heel position. It was the worst time of my life, but unfortunately for my dog I took every single week and we graduated at the top of our class. Once class was over and the jerking ended, Sable never was very reliable in anything she had "learned" in class.

Around the time Sable and I were finishing up class, I took in a cute, spunky Dalmatian puppy someone could not keep. Max joined my household and I found the local AKC kennel club so I could learn more about the wonderful sport of dogs. I met an Alaskan Malamute breeder who believed in nothing but positive training methods and we became fast friends. We managed to start some training classes that were based on more positive methods, but the majority still felt the only good solution was choke and strangle, ear pinches with your choke collar or a pliers if need be, and harsh corrections. The solution to a "behavior problem" had nothing to do with understanding the triggers for the problem but on "making your dog stop it." Barking was punished by an open fist to the bottom of your dog's muzzle, dogs were to be strung up for lunging or aggressive behavior, and puppy class curriculum included "alpha rolls" and "scruff shaking 101."

During this time I had the opportunity to watch a videotaped seminar given by Leslie Nelson who showed the most enlightening and heartwarming training techniques based solely on positive reinforcement. That was my "ah-ha moment" and I was sold on the fact that the way my mother had taught me to teach our dogs was right. One night after a club meeting (where I was the club's Training Director), I pointed out the horrible trend of 20-30 dogs enrolled and only a handful toughing it out. I was told "who cares if they stay as long as the check clears." I decided to venture out on my own and teach positive training in classes with limited numbers offering a more individualized program. I truly wanted to help people teach their dogs what their expectations were.

I never looked back. My classes were full, my clients were happy, their dogs were happy and the kennel club asked me to resign as I was hurting their program. I happily walked out the door with a huge sigh of relief.

Since 1997, I have been offering classes and private lessons to people in the hopes of helping them deal with all means of canine chaos, and helping them create from the start the well-mannered dog they want. I did my best to toss out the old mentality and did not offer "obedience" classes but training classes — after all I was training the trainers, not the dogs.

I have titled numerous dogs in different venues, but have found working with the average dog owner and teaching my own dogs new things to be greatly rewarding. My dogs and I have learned and grown together and because of them I am the trainer I am today, for without their quirks and personalities I would never have had to learn so much, nor had the opportunity to enjoy, the great bonds and partnerships we have shared.

Chapter One

Learning Concepts

Controlling behavior through consequences

All behavior produces consequences, and is a product of them. Simply put, when your dog does something, something happens (naturally or contrived), which increases or decreases the likelihood of the behavior in the future.

If you call your dog to you and cause something unpleasant to happen, the likelihood of him coming to you in the future decreases as he will try to avoid this unpleasant experience in the future. Likewise, if your dog gets to you and cookies, games and/or attention appear, he will be more likely to come when called in the future as he will seek out the pleasant experience.

Consequences are either naturally occurring or contrived, but always happen; think "for every action there is a reaction."

By managing or controlling the consequences you can better control your dog's behavior. If you want your dog to respond to you in distracting situations, make sure the best consequence is you, as consequences can also be competing with one another.

For example, at the dog park, the dog has many consequence options; he can come to you when called (and potentially have to leave the park) or blow you off to play with another dog, roll in something lovely, chase squirrels, gain attention from a fellow dog parker and more. It is your job to make your dog see you as the best option there is.

Understanding reinforcement

Reinforcement is any consequence that increases the likelihood a behavior will repeat in the future. Reinforcement must be something your dog actually perceives as worth gaining enough to want to work for it. What may seem reinforcing to you may not be to your dog. For example, dogs as a general rule do not like to be hugged or in some cases petted or touched at all, so the use of petting such a dog for reinforcement would not work, even though you find it enjoyable.

The most recognized form of reinforcement is positive reinforcement. *Positive reinforcement* is adding something that increases the likelihood a behavior will be performed again in the future. When your dog comes to you, you give him a treat or play a game with him, the likelihood of him coming to you in the future goes up (assuming he likes the treat or game).

Your job is to find those reinforcers your dog will happily work for. Reinforcement has gotten a bad rap as being all about cookie training, which is simply not true; it is about finding what is reinforcing enough to your dog to make him want to work for it.

Learning in dogs

It is important that you do not compare your dog's progress to that of the other dogs. Some dogs (much like some people) will catch on faster to the skills being asked of them, while others may need more time to digest and make the associations needed. All dogs have the capacity to learn and become great companions. Certain breeds of dogs are generally easier to train as they are more biddable (willing to work with you), while other breeds are generally bred to be more independent thinking, and others yet are simply hard to motivate to do anything; and this is not even consistent within a breed itself. Be sure to understand your breed (or the mixes therein) to better understand his thinking. Golden Retrievers are very biddable and bred to work with people (and have stuff in their mouths) while Dalmatians were bred to be independent thinking/working dogs that chased away intruders and were to guard their humans property, but each dog is an individual with his own traits and learning curve.

Age and length of ownership (and location) are also factors to your dog's learning curve. A new puppy is not only sucking up stimuli like a sponge, but has no behavior history so is ripe for learning appropriate behaviors right from the start. A dog new to your home is also more likely to be receptive to learning what is appropriate in his new setting, but this must be done from the start. Trying to set rules mid-game just will not work well, you need to begin before old behavior patterns begin in his new location.

Your dog may not learn in an organized and orderly fashion. Learning does not happen in a straight line, but rather in spurts and setbacks. You will also find your dog go through testing periods. Sometimes your dog can seemingly forget what he has learned, add his own creative flair or just plain lose interest in performing a well worked behavior. Not only is this normal, but it can be a sign your dog is ready to learn more complex behaviors.

An extended sit with lots of distractions is a complex behavior, especially when doing it duo!

You have been promoted — management here you come
Management is essentially setting your dog (and yourself, for that matter) up for success. It is being proactive and creating an environment in which your dog is going to thrive, where behavior is more likely to be appropriate, and where confusion and blurring of the lines is reduced or eliminated.

Exercise
One often over looked and underutilized management tool is *exercise*. Many dogs with behavior issues are actually lacking proper physical and mental stimulation. Many dogs spend the majority of their time home alone, possibly in a crate and get very little physical exercise. This lends itself well to destructive or other inappropriate behaviors.

Walking your dog somewhere where he can be off-lead is an excellent means of exercise (I do not mean the dog park). You can hike about as your dog is allowed to run, burning up some pent up energy and can learn to check-in with you. Take some treats with you and every time your dog returns to you say "check-in" and hand him a treat, this will teach him to be near you when he hears "check-in" and also helps your dog to find being near you a good thing (making him more likely to continue to do so).

Hide and seek is another game to add to your hike. This fun game also keeps your dog checking in with you and adds some mental stimulation. As your dog is running around with his back to you,

An extended sit with lots of distractions is a complex behavior, especially when doing it duo! Photo © Thomas Photography

simply step off the trail; when he looks back, he will not see you and should begin to search. If your dog has no issues with your disappearance, you may have a relationship issue to work on. Be sure you are in a safe place with your dog and that he is not a runner. Remember, you are setting your dog up for success and using management, so do not set your dog up to run off or totally ignore you. A dog park is not ideal for this as it offers your dog too many choices.

Couch potato exercise is possible with the following games:

Tug of War: Regardless of what you have read, tug of war does not cause aggression. When done correctly it can actually teach your dog to honor rules, to operate with self/impulse-control and to be more responsive and respectful to you as his leader. The rules of tug of war must be very clearly defined and consistent each session.

They should be:

- Your dog is to release the tug object upon cue or the game ends.

- Your dog must sit or lie down to resume the game.

- You must be consistent with the rules.

In addition to the tug, part you can also add some retrieve. If your dog fails to return the toy to you, the game ends. It is not your job to go chasing the dog or the toy.

Hide and seek: A little more off the couch for you, but you can quietly hide in different parts of the house while your dog attempts to find you.

For the more couch potato version, you can hide your dogs kibble all over a room or two and allow him to hunt for his meal. This is good mental stimulation.

Fetch it up: This game can be played when you are dog tired and just want to lie down and relax. Simply roll or toss a ball (or other toy) around the room, down the hall or elsewhere. The rule is simple, the dog shows up with the ball/toy or the game ends. Your dog will soon understand the rule and happily play along. While not all dogs/puppies are natural retrievers, they can all be taught to do so and to enjoy it.

Keep away — the human version: This game takes two or more humans who can pass the ball, toy, treat or other beloved object around preventing the dog from getting it, with breaks of "Yay you get it" for the dog. This game can be used to create a recall. Call the dog's name and say "here" when you are the one with the toy and are going to give it up to the dog. Each person can take turns with this and either call and reinforce every time, or use a very intermittent schedule of call and play.

Keep away — the canine version: This game is controlled by the dog who very easily teaches his owner to chase him all around when he has forbidden objects. This would not be the version to play or get sucked into.

Socialization

Socialization is another important management tool. While the window for socializing slams shut by around 16 weeks of age, it is not locked. This means socializing an older puppy or adult dog is more complicated than taking out your 8-16 week old puppy, but it can (and should) be done.

Socialization is about getting your dog out to experience as many novel situations as possible. This includes different people (men, women, young children, teens, boys, girls, hats, beards, glasses, tall, short, fat, thin and so on), different surfaces (grass, concrete, carpet, hardwood, tile), different environmental situations (city, country, subdivision), trips to the veterinarian for social calls (and the groomer) and about anything you can imagine in a POSITIVE way. Allow your dog to experience at his own pace, never force your dog to meet or experience anything as this may actually backfire.

Behavior Management

Some *behavior management*, (dog communication style) goes a long way, meaning you control the resources. Control of resources is for the leader. Resources you can control include food, toys, places (sleeping areas, rooms, and so on), his body (grooming, handling, personal space, restraint), and reproduction.

> A word on dominance. Dominance is tossed around frequently (and on popular TV shows) as a personality trait. It is actually a relationship between two or more beings based on context and resources. A dog (or a human, or a pig or a fish) is not a dominant being, but can at any one time be in a position of dominance by controlling a resource. If a dog gives up a beloved item to another dog — it does not mean he was dominated, it simply means he was willing to let it go. Too many behaviors are incorrectly labeled as the dog trying to dominate the owner and do nothing to address the actual behavior problem.

Back to control of resources. In the animal kingdom, it is a normal and natural consequence. Have you ever watched wolves or other large animals of prey at feeding time? Very clearly there is a hierarchy of feeding. There is no fighting, no physical corrections or "alpha rolling," just communication and the natural order. Your job is to be in charge of food and feeding. Never allow a dog to free feed or graze, as it does not allow you to control the resource. A free fed dog understands when he wants food he has food and magical food fairies always make sure he does. He does not have to really offer you any respect because you have no control of this very important resource (from his point of view). Feed your dog one or more times per day with a measured amount of his food.

Food

Ditch the dish: If you feed your dog a commercial kibble you can actually use this as training time treats (at home more so than in a class), by working with your dog on behaviors you like. You can also choose to use his food for mental stimulation and offer him food puzzles or food dispensing toys, play the hide and seek game, or feed him entirely by hand as you run through a slew of manners exercises. At any rate, you should be the one who controls when and how he eats (as well as what).

Places

It is your job to set rules about the use of places. Places include the rooms in your house, your yard, sleeping spaces, furniture and your vehicle (there are more of course but these are the main ones), and you determine what access (if any) your dog has. This can be achieved with management techniques such as crates, gates, fences, tethers, doors and simply setting the 'no go' rule from day one. This should then be set in stone — black and white so as to not give your dog mixed messages. Part of this includes making sure your dog cannot access "off limit areas" when you are not home. Anytime your dog can access them when you are away, he learns it is ok when you are gone and not ok when you are there.

Handling

You should be able to handle, restrain, groom or simply pet your dog as needed. This does not mean you should hug and squeeze and restrain him for the pure enjoyment of it. You do need to respect his boundaries. You should be able to apply medications, or give pills, inspect body parts and other normal care situations without issue.

Behavior Markers

Behavior markers are secondary reinforcement (the conditioned reinforcer) as they are neutral until paired with a primary reinforcer (a biologically programmed reinforcement) such as food. The secondary or conditioned reinforcer marks the behavior and lets your dog know reinforcement is coming.

When teaching your dog what is appropriate, you must be able to communicate to him what behavior is desired. You want to mark it so he can make the correct choices. Behavior marking can be verbal (YES) or some mechanical device (a training clicker, bell, whistle). I suggest the use of both.

Training clickers come in a wide variety of styles and shapes. I personally prefer the original box style clicker which is a rectangle shaped, plastic box with a small metal tab that makes a metallic clicking sound when depressed. According to Karen Pryor in her book *Reaching the Animal Mind,* a clicker works by tapping into the amygdale (the part of the brain shown to perform a primary role in the processing and memory of emotional responses). Essentially causing the body to take a snap shot of what the muscles are doing at the time of the click. With a few repetitions (using correct timing) your dog's brain is able to determine what specific muscle movements were responsible for the click and forth-coming reinforcement.

Verbal markers are words used at the time of the behavior. I use the verbal marker "Yes" other people use "Good" or "Good Dog." Both forms of marking are acceptable means of teaching, although the clicker has many advantages over verbal marking for certain target behaviors.

Behavior markers are only needed for the acquisition stage of learning. They are no longer needed once your dog understands what the correct behavior is. This means your dog is performing it on cue reliably (80%).

When using a behavior marker; primary reinforcement needs to follow shortly, so the click does not lose its effectiveness.

Timing is important when using a behavior marker as you do not want to mark and reinforce the wrong behavior.

It's all sounds to them
Dogs' brains are not programmed for verbal human language. They do not understand words. It is a biological reality. They do however, have the ability to associate sounds to behavior. Human verbal language is to your dog a sound. You must keep this in mind when you are deciding what words you will use to cue a behavior.

Since dogs are making sound-behavior associations, there can be no dual meanings for any word. In other words down cannot mean to lie down and to get off of something; one word, one behavior. Because we as a species love to talk, we confuse our dogs on a daily basis and wonder what went wrong when they do not comply with our wishes.

It is also important to remember one behavior equals one clear verbal cue. Sit is sit, sit down is sit then down not sit, using this phrase and interchanging with sit is confusing and will leave your dog doing nothing.

What are you doing — target behaviors and planning
A plan also ensures you are accomplishing something as you know what your target behavior is. It is a good problem-solving tool not only for dealing with a behavior you wish to teach, but also in working on removing a behavior you would like to disappear.

Have a plan when working with your dog. Know what you want to accomplish and how you will get there. Describe the behavior you want, do not simply say "I want my dog to lie down". What is involved? What does it look like? How does he get there? When you do this you are better able to reinforce any small steps to the behavior if need be (this would be the use of approximations). When teaching your dog to lie down, you may discover he will not simply put his body in a down position. To help him you will need to reinforce the small behaviors that happen between the stand/sit and being in prone position which can include hunching over to get the treat while keeping his butt on the ground.

The Power of Ten
A quick training exercise...
Get 10 treats for your dog — have in your hand
Lure dog into a behavior with treats in hand
Give one treat when behavior happens
Repeat 9 more times

Get 10 treats for your dog — in your pocket
Lure dog into a behavior with one treat in your hand
Give treat for correct behavior
Get another treat-repeat the above
Only reinforce for correct behavior

Get 10 treats for your dog in your pocket
Lure dog into behavior — no treat in hand
When correct behavior happens get one treat out of pocket-reinforce (can say Yes or click to mark)
Repeat 9 more times

Take a break — Play Play Play

Get 10 treats for your dog — in your pocket
Lure dog into behavior
Add verbal cue when behavior happens
Get treat out — reinforce
repeat 9 more times

Get out 10 treats for your dog in your pocket
Say cue
Wait 1/2 a sec or so, lure into behavior
Reinforce — repeat 9 more times

Get out 10 treats for your dog-in hand
Say cue
WAIT, WITH NO WORDS!
If dog gives you the behavior
Rapid fire the ten treats one at a time!
YAY!
If not...go back one step — repeat and move forward...

When training using the Power of Ten, the number of treats need not be 10; you can decide to use 5 throughout the process. You may also take breaks between any of the steps to play or relax, so do not feel you must do all steps at once.

Practice the Power of Ten using sit as the behavior.

Training Exercises

Attention

One of the first things you want your dog to master is eye contact and attention. Direct eye contact can be (for some dogs) very difficult as it is actually confrontational canine behavior. Once a dog is conditioned to do so and understands it is the beginning of good things, it makes teaching sessions less stressful.

It is safe to say if you do not have the attention of your audience, your message may not get through. How often have you caught yourself moving your attention away from someone who is talking to you? How much did you get from the conversation? When your dog is focused on you, giving you eye contact, and his full attention he is ready to work with you and to take in what you are teaching.

Attention and eye contact can also be used to help your dog focus when stressed, afraid or nervous. If you are working on desensitizing him to something, you can have him look to you when the stressor is present instead of reacting to it.

To teach this you simply hold a treat at or near your eyes, using the old "pork chop around the neck" to get him to play theory. When your dog looks at or toward your face, mark and reinforce (YES or click and give him the treat). Once your dog is looking at or toward you reliably, move the food away from your face. Hold your arm out perpendicular to your body and wait, when his eyes shift toward your face mark and reinforce. Repeat this process until you can have your dog looking at you for several minutes before marking and reinforcing. At this point, you can add a verbal cue such as "Watch me" or something you will remember easily. You will get the behavior, say the verbal cue and reinforce (the marker is no longer needed when the dog is performing the behavior reliably on cue and past the initial acquisition stage).

Sit on verbal cue

This motion should encourage your dog to look up at the treat and follow it with his nose, which will (in most cases) cause him to put his butt on the ground.

To add the verbal cue, you must make sure your dog is reliably sitting (with the hand motion). Once you are able to get your dog into a sit 8 out of 10 times reliably you can add your cue. As your dog sits, say "Sit", mark and reinforce.

Default behavior

When you are not offering your dog any communication he should not be free to just do as he wants (unless you have released him to do so). He should be offering a default behavior that is his "between" communication behavior.

Some dogs that default to a sit and others that default to a down; either is fine, as is a stand. The goal is the dog is near me and waiting for the next communication.

Reinforce your dog for eye contact or looking toward your face.

Sit on verbal cue

To teach the sit hold a treat in your hand at your dog's nose.

Slowly move your treat back and over your dog's head.

When you are standing around, with your dog on a lead, wait for him to offer a behavior such a sit or down, then mark and reinforce. It is very important you do not cue your dog. He has to make a choice and offer the behavior with no prompting from you. If you tell your dog what to do instead of defaulting to a behavior he will simply wait for you to tell him what to do. This may be fine while he is on lead, but will not work well once you try for off lead control later.

Introducing your marker

For your behavior marker to work, you must first help your dog associate it with the primary reinforcement. To begin you will be using treats as they are the typically more enticing and motivating when dealing with competing reinforcers.

This is needed for use of a mechanical marker so your dog can make the connection between the marker and the incoming reinforcement.

Simply use your marker (click), wait approximately 1/2 a second then offer your dog the reinforcement. Repeat 10 times, take a small break then do another 10 repetitions, take a small break then 10 more. Put your marker away for a brief period then pull it out and repeat. You should begin to notice your dog having a reaction to the sound of the clicker now as he understands the sound means a treat.

If your dog is afraid of the clicker either find a soft click or use a verbal marker.

For fun, (and a challenge) use a tennis ball to work on timing. Try to mark (click-Yes") when the ball hits the floor.

Chapter One Behaviors Log

Skill	Date	Date	Date	Date	Date	Date	Date	Date
Attention								
Sit on Verbal Cue								
Default Behavior								
Introduce Marker								
Training Notes:								

How to use this log: Train using a set number of treats per session and mark down how many treats you actually use in a session. Example — session 1 dog received 5 treats for 5 correct responses

Chapter Two

Learning Concepts

Catching desired behaviors

It is time to let go of old behavior patterns (including your own), and move from punishing undesired behaviors to catching and reinforcing desired behaviors. This concept will feel foreign and may even feel as if it is more work, but it will soon become your new behavior pattern.

When you begin to focus on and reinforce the behaviors you like, your dog will begin to offer you more and more of it. I routinely let my dogs know they did a good thing by marking the behavior with "good choices" and giving them some much wanted attention.

It is a very simple concept, but a very powerful one. Catch your dog (spouse, child) being right.

Real world consequences

Food is not necessary as reinforcement in all cases and is not the only form of reinforcement. Many external (and internal) stimuli can work as reinforcement. An excellent example is barking at passersby. Your dog barks like mad in the window and the passerby, well, passes by. Your dog is reinforced (internally and externally) by making the stranger go away. This behavior is reinforced over and over and over making it a very strong behavior, and one that can be hard to extinguish.

Most unwanted behaviors are a direct result of real world consequences reinforcing them. To best end an undesirable behavior, you must first figure out what is maintaining it.

Jumping up is a common behavior that is reinforced by real-world or naturally occuring consequences. Dog owners most often want to stop the behavior. What usually happens is that your dog jumps up, and you unwittingly give him attention, thinking you are actually correcting it. Common corrections to jumping include grabbing your dog's paws, pushing him off or talking to him. These can actually be very reinforcing to your dog.

Fading the food lure

When you first begin teaching your dog a behavior you will be using a very high rate of reinforcement, giving a treat for every correct response. It is very important that you move away from this reinforcement schedule as quickly as possible and move to a variable schedule of reinforcement. (*Variable reinforcement* is variable; meaning the dog (or training subject) cannot predict which correct performance will be the one that earns the reinforcement. Variable reinforcement should be done completely random so as to not create a pattern. Dogs are excellent at figuring out patterns. An example of a pattern would be one treat, no treat, one treat, no treat. An example of random reinforcement would look like this a treat, 5 repetitions without treats, 2 with, 1 without, 10 with, 5 without, 1 with, 4 without, 2 with, 10 without. This pattern is difficult to predict so the dog cannot anticipate when he is going to see reinforcement.)

When you first begin teaching an exercise (acquisition stage), you should have treats in your hand, I recommend 10 treats for 10 trials. By doing so, you have treats at the ready to reinforce immediately.

After the initial acquisition stage, it is vital you move away from this continuous schedule of reinforcement or your dog will become dependent on the treat and the behaviors will drop in reliability. You must be careful not to do so too quickly either.

To begin get one treat in your hand and lure your dog into the position you are working on — mark and treat. Next, lure your dog again, same hand no treat. If he performs the behavior then mark and get him a treat from your bait bag (or pocket). Continue to alternate between food lure and empty hand trial. Be sure to be random so your dog cannot predict when there will or will not be a treat in hand. You are working on fading out the food in your hand.

If your dog will not do the behavior exercise with an empty hand trial, then simply walk to a new spot, wait a few seconds than do a treat lured exercise before ending that particular session. Be sure you have given your dog the opportunity to respond to the empty hand trial before using food.

Continue to work on fading the lure each training session so you can catch your dog when he is ready to move to that next level.

Using jackpots

A jackpot is a special reinforcer. It can be a special and unusual treat or a large amount of a regular treat (it can also be a fun and special game or toy). A favorite jackpot of my dogs is cheese, as it really makes a great impression.

A jackpot can be presented as that super special something (cheese) or to simply give a handful of the treats from your bait bag instead of just one. When using a jackpot with a behavior marker you need only mark once. More marking does not give any more information.

Jackpots can be used in several ways and can be very useful in training. You may want to use a jackpot when your dog is working in a particularly distracting situation, or when your dog makes a breakthrough and begins to perform an exercise that has been difficult.

Jackpots make memorable impressions. If your dog anticipates a jackpot is possible, he will work harder (and better). Jackpots help keep training interesting and relevant to your dog; they are like a bonus.

Training Exercises

Attention

You should work on attention in two ways this week. First, use a food lure to get your dog to look at your face or give you direct eye contact. You can begin to slowly increase the amount of time your dog must look at your face (eye contact) before you mark and reinforce. Between each trial, move to a slightly different location. If your dog looks away before you mark and reinforce, take a small break, move slightly and start again, lowering your time expectation.

Second, randomly catch your dog looking at you, mark it and reinforce. You are not trying to elicit or lure attention here. You are just catching it when it happens. You can use your verbal marker and anything your dog finds reinforcing (YES and some attention or a quick game). The more often you catch attention, the more your dog will start to offer it.

Leave it

Approximation #1: Put your dog on his leash and toss a treat on the floor behind you. When your dog moves toward the treat, body block by stepping between him and the treat. When your dog looks up at you, away from the treat, or stops attempting to move towards it, step back out of the way. Before your dog can attempt to get it mark and reinforce from your bait bag (pick up the treat from the floor). Repeat for a total of 10 trials. The goal is for your dog to make no move toward the treat on the floor when he has access and to look to you when something inviting is available.

Approximation #2: Get a treat your dog really likes and set it on the floor. When your dog attempts to grab it, cover it with your hand (or foot). When your dog looks at you or away from the treat mark and reinforce (pick the treat up off the floor) by giving a treat to your dog from your bait bag. Repeat this for a total of 10 trials.

Approximation #3: Set up treats or toys on the floor or some surface. Put your dog on his lead and walk him by the treats/toys so he is just out of reach. Do not jerk or pull on the leash. Let the dog make the choice to look away (to you), mark and reinforce with a treat in your bait bag or with a toy. Be sure you keep your dog at a distance that does not allow him to gain access to the "off limits" items.
Repeat this for a total of 10 trials.

Loose lead walking — the pre-heeling behavior

Before you can begin teaching the fine art of "heeling" your dog must understand how to walk with a loose leash. The length of the leash is not relevant as your dog must understand to walk with slack in all situations.

To start your dog working on leash with you, attach your leash and hold on to the end, letting your dog have the slack or most of it. Do not hold the leash tight removing any slack. This will only teach your dog to operate without slack, at the end of a tight leash (with a lot of pressure on the throat). The dog will walk at the end of a lead 1 foot or 100 feet with this method. Get a favorite toy or treat and begin to walk backwards as you call your dog's name. Every time your dog gets to you give him the treat or a quick play with the toy and keep moving backwards. You are reinforcing your dog moving with you on a slack or loose lead. Walking backwards works well as dogs like to follow or chase things and they are more likely to walk toward you (since you are facing them).

If your dog rushes past you or does not follow, try being more interesting by adding unusual sounds, running backwards, jumping up and down, and so on. Then reinforce him for being near you. The goal is to get your dog to walk in the same direction you are without pulling or pressure from the collar. If you need to, body block your dog.

Once your dog is following you reliably you want to reinforce him for being alongside you. You will continue to walk backwards but instead of reinforcing for getting to you, you will turn and reinforce while your dog is alongside you. The goal is to keep your dog walking on a loose lead with you. Reinforce your dog for being in the correct place. You will immediately turn back and keep walking backwards then turning to reinforce.

After some reliable repetitions you can begin walking forward with your dog. You only reinforce when your dog is near enough to get the treat from you. Do not reinforce by leaning to your dog. Your dog needs to get to the correct position himself.

Remember that loose lead walking is not heeling. It is simply walking on the leash with slack and no pulling, or lunging. Heeling can only be taught once your dog is reliable at loose leash walking, otherwise you are asking too much at one time. There is no real verbal cue in this stage of teaching your dog (but terms such as "Easy" or "Walk Nice" can be used). You should encourage and talk to your dog to keep him interested and engaged. I also suggest you start in a low distraction area, such as your own home. You can attach the leash and let it drag as you lead your dog around. Make it fun, make a game of it, the more fun it is the more likely your dog is to want to keep playing.

Recall — chase

You want to practice motivated recalls. The goal is to increase your dog's desire to get to you as quickly as possible. You are not working on anything but your dog getting to you fast and happy so do not worry about using any sit-stays; it will slow your dog down, lower his motivation and if your dog does not stay you are setting him up for failure on that exercise. You can work on simply calling your dog at random times when he is going about the business of being your dog.

Chase recalls: Run away from your dog calling him enthusiastically, by name as you go (do not use the cue "come" or "here" — you are only working on behavior at this point). Run about 10-15 feet, (turn), mark/reinforce your dog for being there.

Chase recalls

Running backwards encourages your dog to chase you.

Reinforce for getting to you.

Begin to add your verbal cue when your dog arrives, then treat.

Toy chase recall: Find your dog's favorite toy, tease him with it then run away calling your dog's name enthusiastically. Stop, turn to face your dog with your feet shoulder width apart and toss the toy between your legs so the dog needs to run between your legs to get the toy (going through you).

Play with your dog using the toy. Make it a game of tug and retrieve so your dog coming to you is highly reinforcing and fun. This is a great bonding experience and helps your dog to see that getting to you is a good thing.

Note: in both versions you are not using any verbal recall cue.

Name response

Work on getting your dog to respond when you say his name. Remember simply saying his name is not a cue to do any other behavior and should not be looked at as such. In other words, if you say your dog's name, do not expect him to come to you or sit or anything other than look to you. His name is the signal he should be paying attention to you and ready for information.

The goal is for your dog to look toward you when you say his name. Say his name one time and wait for a response. Do not continue to call his name if you are getting no response. Simply stop and try again later.

Begin working in a low distraction area. Say your dog's name. When he turns to you mark and reinforce. Be sure to vary your reinforcement between treats, toys, games and simple praise.

Handling

All dogs must be able to be handled and in some cases safely restrained. This week before giving your dog his food begin to handle his feet, check his ears and hold his muzzle. If your dog does not allow this, simply put his food away and try again in a few minutes. He will begin to learn allowing you to touch him will get him his food.

You can also work on playing with your dog's feet as a game. The goal is for your dog to become comfortable being handled.

To begin working on restraint, hold your dog's collar in one hand while he is standing and place your opposite open, flat hand on his hip applying slight pressure. Your dog is to remain standing without moving (all four feet should be still) and he should relax (a sigh, open mouth and light panting, for example). The reinforcement for this exercise is you releasing his collar and standing up.

In addition to the above exercises look at doing some massage or TTouch® with your dog. These are simple hands on experiences that will help your dog adjust to the handling and touch that so often is a part of the human-dog relationship.

Chapter Two Behaviors Log

Skill	Date	Date	Date	Date	Date	Date	Date	Date	Date	Date
Leave It										
Approximation #1										
Approximation #2										
Approximation #3										
Loose Lead Walking										
Recall-Chase										
Chase										
Toy Chase										
Name Response										
Handling										
Training Notes:										

How to use this log: Train using a set number of treats per session and mark down how many treats you actually use in a session. Example — session 1 dog received 5 treats for 5 correct responses

Chapter Three

Learning Concepts

Positive solutions for behavior issues

From time to time your dog will exhibit behaviors you have concern with (barking, digging, jumping up, chewing, and so on). First it is important to remember that these are normal dog behaviors. They are not a problem for the dog — they are human behavior problems. That being said, you can teach your dog that these behaviors are unacceptable, and in some cases how to perform an appropriate version of them.

Differential Reinforcement of an incompatible behavior
Use of this teaching method requires you to step outside the box so to speak and look at your dog's behaviors in an entirely new light. Instead of concentrating on a behavior you do not like, such as jumping all over people, you will look at the problem from a new angle. What is a behavior your dog can do that is incompatible with jumping up? To curb your dog's relentless need to jump all over you and your guests simply teach him to sit (and stay) instead. Ignore the jumping and begin to replace it with a sit. This is an incompatible behavior you can shape and create, even to the point your doorbell can cue the dog to sit quietly.

Getting creative — a time and place for everything
There are behaviors that you are better off just conceding. You can still lose the battle but win the war. Dogs enjoy digging and destruction. It is fun. One way to allow your dog to continue to enjoy his much needed doggyness is to create "dog zones" where he is allowed to simply be a dog. When doing so, be sure you establish rules for their use.

Digging dog zone — Set up a sandbox for your dog. You can buy, borrow or build one that is safe, dog friendly and a place he can call his own. When you catch your dog digging in an unacceptable area, simply move him to his sandbox. Let him know it is ok to play and dig here. This will save your yard, garden and flower bed; yet still allow him to dig. Most times owners can manage to suppress the digging only to create a new behavior issue somewhere else. If he needs the outlet he needs the outlet — make it happen.

Doggy destruction zone — Chew it up, Chew it up, Way up – your dog needs to "kill" stuff and tear it up and make it garbage for the sheer joy (and innate need) of it. One way to allow him his moments is to create them.

Once a week (or a day or a month) give your dog something he can just tear up. My dogs love to destruct paper towel and toilet paper tubes — so I just let them. Why should I battle their need to chew up stuff when I can just give them their own?

You can also create a doggy rumpus room if you prefer they not be doggish in the house. Create an area for them full of things they can tear up — a box of Kleenex, cardboard, pull apart toys and more. You will simply send your dog to his designated area where you will give him his tear it up stuff. Be sure you are in control of this situation. Your dog only gets cardboard or paper you give him. He cannot just take it at will. You set up his chew room and allow access to it.

Make it go away — extinction
Extinction is the process of getting rid of unwanted behavior by removing the reinforcement for it (this does not mean adding punishment). Extinction works because behaviors that are no longer reinforced tend to die a natural death.

Many unwanted dog behaviors are actually maintained by the owner's attention, remove the attention the behavior will go away. Dogs are excellent at attention seeking behaviors and train their owners well; dog barks, barks, barks relentlessly and you drop what you are doing. My old dog Indigo (bless his soul) would stand in the kitchen and make this bizarre bark, moan, grumble noise. The first time it happened I wondered what on earth is that dog doing now? My husband emerged from his office, went to refrigerator, took out a hot dog, handed it to Indigo and went back to the office. Now how is that for a great trainer? Indigo had my hubby trained well. I would not give him what he wanted and he learned there was no reason to perform this behavior if only I was home.

Some behaviors can be put on extinction by simply ignoring them, more dangerous behaviors may require the help of a professional behavior consultant, and some may just need a combination of ignore and differential reinforcement.

When putting a behavior on extinction, beware of the extinction burst. This is where the behavior gets worse, escalates and hits a record high, before it finally comes down and disappears. Be tough, hold strong and do not cave to the burst. If you do you will actually have reinforced the new bigger version of the unwanted behavior.

Reinforcement schedules

In a nut-shell and for purposes of this manual, you will be using a fixed schedule of reinforcement and a variable schedule of reinforcement.

Fixed schedule of reinforcement is predictable and in the acquisition stages you will use a 1 to 1 ratio (one correct performance = one reinforcement) known as a continuous schedule. As your dog becomes reliable in performance and seems to fully understand the task at hand, you will move to a variable schedule of reinforcement.

Variable reinforcement is variable; meaning the dog (or training subject) cannot predict which correct performance will be the one that earns the reinforcement. Variable reinforcement should be done completely random so as to not create a pattern. Dogs are excellent at figuring out patterns. An example of a pattern would be one treat, no treat, one treat, no treat. An example of random reinforcement would look like this a treat, 5 repetitions without treats, 2 with, 1 without, 10 with, 5 without, 1 with, 4 without, 2 with, 10 without. This pattern is difficult to predict so the dog cannot anticipate when he is going to see reinforcement.

Variable reinforcement when done correctly is actually the best at maintaining behaviors; think about gamblers. Even though they may not win frequently or at all in a session, they keep coming back because as some point they do win and that fuels the fire. Once your dog is reliable with a behavior you want to move to this variable schedule and slowly fade the lure.

Setting criteria — duration, distance, distraction

As your dog becomes proficient at the basic behaviors you are going to want to make changes to the criteria of the behaviors. Three common criteria are duration, distance and distraction.

Duration refers to time. Duration is the first component you will want to raise when teaching any behavior. It will be much easier for you to get your dog to hold his behavior for an extended length of time before trying to add distance.

Distance is the amount of physical space between you and your dog while working on a behavior. You cannot expect your dog to sit while you walk half a county away, you will need to slowly and systematically increase distance.

Distractions are those things going on externally (and/or internally) that you are competing with when working with your dog. It is always best to start working in as a low a distraction area as possible and slowly adding more distractions as you become successful with each session. Very clearly group training classes offer a distraction challenge for many dogs and their owners, keep this in mind when working.

It is my experience that the order in which criteria should be raised is duration, distance, and then distraction. As a general rule getting duration will ease your dog into distance as he is already able to hold a position for an extended period of time.

Do not rush your dog or any of the criteria. The goal is to set your dog up for success.

Keeping it real — expectations

There is a concept in learning theory referred to as errorless training. Errorless training refers to setting up each training session so that your subject (in this case your dog) never makes a mistake. Realistic expectations allow you to set your dog up for success.

It is your job as your dog's teacher to learn how to read your dog and see things from his point of view. Mistakes reflect on the teacher not the student and can mean you are asking too much. You need to anticipate situations in which your dog might have trouble learning or performing. After nearly 10 years of competing in the conformation (dog show) ring with my Australian Shepherd, Trivia, I decided to begin competing in Rally Obedience. I taught her the exercises and added distractions; some so crazy they would never happen in competition. The day of her first trial we totally bombed. I, as her coach, never considered how conditioned she was to dog showing, so did not include working her in a dog show scenario to help her understand we were doing a new sport in essentially the same environment. While dogs can certainly compete in more than one sport at the same time, the length of time she had spent doing one sport in this environment stuck for her.

> Unrealistic expectations regarding how fast your dog can learn or how reliable his behaviors can be lead to failures. Too many failures lead to confusion for the dog and can be upsetting for both dog and owner, work on small success and build up. You may not always see the progress in learning. Do not let your desire for tangible results lead you to pushing too hard. You may not see any notable changes in any one training session, but learning is happening.

Try creating a training journal or log where you write down your goals, your successes, your failures with dates and times and other conditions (treats used, location and so forth). This will allow you to actually "see" where you are moving forward or may need to make a change to your plan. A journal will allow you to look back and see how far you have come.

Training Exercises

Down from a sit

Down

Practice the down from a sit and from a stand. Remember to do this without a verbal cue as you are trying to get a reliable performance of the behavior.

From a sit: when you have your dog in a sit, hold a treat at his nose, move the treat straight down to his front feet (do not take it out and away, but *straight down from his nose*) and give him about 1/2 a second to follow it. If you have been unable to get your dog down at this point, as long as his butt is still on the floor, mark and reinforce. Some dogs need to be taught to down by approximations. All dogs can lie down, they do it several times a day, doing it for someone on request is not normal, so keep that in mind. After 10 repetitions of hunching forward and remaining in a sit, raise your criteria and expect the dog to move farther forward while remaining in a sit by sliding the treat on the floor from his feet forward, repeat 10 times.

As you may (or may not) guess, you are going to continue to break down the exercise by increasing the distance you can slide the treat before marking and reinforcing. The one constant is your dog must keep his butt on the floor. If he does not, no mark, no treat and go back to where he was successful and move forward again. In this manner you should be able to get your dog lying down which you will jackpot with 10 rapid-fire treats.

From a stand: while your dog is standing use the same approximate treat to nose down to floor and drag so your dog will rock forward until he is in a play bow stance, then slide the treat back under him causing him to rock back and fold into a down. If he is not performing a down, go back and use the same approximations as you did for the sit exercise, but the dog remains standing. Again the only communication you are giving your dog is marking the behavior. Trying to use a verbal behavior cue at this point is only adding to the stress and confusion (for both of you).

Extended sit (down)

This exercise is about adding duration to the sit (down) exercise. It is not a stay. The goal is to have your dog remain in a sit until you release him; using your release cue. Begin by getting your dog to sit. You are free to use a verbal cue if the dog responds to it on the first request, mark and release your dog. Again sit your dog wait 2-5 seconds-mark and release. Continue this pattern increasing the amount of time your dog must sit while you stand in front of your dog close enough to touch is his head (we are not moving away yet) in increments of 2 seconds for each 10 repetitions. Always work in sets of 10, so dog sits for 5 seconds 10 times, than move to 7 seconds, 10 times and so on. Be sure you always mark the behavior (I would use a verbal vs a clicker, as it is crisp, clear and consistent) then give your release cue and the dog gets up — this order is important, as it communicates to the dog that this is the correct behavior, so you may now get up with my permission.

This is pre-stay behavior and your goal is to get your dog to remain in the sit for a minimum of 60 seconds (one minute) without moving, getting up, rearranging, up and back into a sit, shifting etc. If your dog gets up you are to do nothing, walk away no words, no treats nothing and then go back and start again at the duration increment you were last able to accomplish (thirty seconds, ten seconds, however long the last amount of time your dog remained sitting until released by you.)

Stand

Again you are not asking your dog to do something he cannot actually do. You know your dog can stand. The trick is getting your dog to stand when you request he do so and he make the association between the behavior and what you are asking.

Simply begin to move when your dog is on all four feet, mark and reinforce, simple — but not easy.

Position changes

You will be working on position changes based on the behavior exercises your dog can successfully do. Work on having your dog change from sit to down to sit to stand to down. You are still using only luring and will mark the behavior when correct. Each time you work on it begin to raise the criterion by expecting the dog to change positions quicker. To start give him time to think it through and make it happen. Once you note your dog seems to understand the game, only mark and reinforce when he does it within a specified amount of time-such as within 5 seconds and work to immediate response (within ½ a second of your lure).

Go to place

Go to place

The process of getting your dog to use a *go to* is relatively simple, but not necessarily easy. It is a systematic, step-by-step process that takes a small bit of time on your part.

To begin you must first determine what the *go to* is. You can use something like a dog bed, blanket, area rug, or towel to name a few. Begin with a low distraction setting.

The first step of training this exercise is to get your dog to engage with the *go to*. Any interaction your dog has gets marked and reinforced (when your dog does something you like you will say "Yes" or click and give him a treat). What your dog initially does with the *go to* can be simply sniffing it or putting a paw on it. Continue to mark and reinforce this until your dog is actively interacting with the *go to*. At this stage you will need to stand close to your designated *go to*. No verbal cues (commands) are being used at this time.

Once your dog gets the game, you can raise your criteria (what is expected by your dog as correct behavior). The goal now is to get your dog to offer a different behavior. This could be putting all four feet on the *go to* or sitting if already standing on it. Try to get this to happen without luring or giving a cue. You want your dog to think and to create a default behavior. If your dog is simply not getting it, you can lure one or two times, then wait again to see if he offers the behavior. This leap to new behavior takes patience on your part. Each time your dog offers the new behavior you will mark and reinforce (on the go to).

Once this new behavior is reliable (8 out of 10 attempts correct) you will work on raising the criteria again. The ultimate goal is to get your dog to lie down on the *go to* when he hears the doorbell ring or a knock at the door (there are other times you will want this as well, and you should be able to work through those scenarios as well).

Once your dog is going to the *go to* and lying down, begin to increase the distance between yourself and the *go to*. Move in small increments (move a few inches at a time) away from the *go to*. If you move too far away too fast your dog may not get the behavior. Generally as you work away from the *go to*, your dog will want to offer the behavior near you and not on the *go to*, so be ready to move back toward it a bit and reinforce when your dog gets on it (the *go to*). You want to be able to get your dog going to the go to from further away from the *go to*.

Adding cues is done once your dog is reliably going to the *go to* and offering the behavior of choice (down for example). What you say is limited only by your imagination. Use something you will remember for your verbal cue. Generally "Go To" or "Spot" work well, but use what works for you. You will also want to work with an *environmental cue*, or EC, (something that occurs naturally around your dog that triggers the go to behavior). A perfect EC is the doorbell.

Adding your doorbell (door knock) takes a small bit of retraining (and potentially a second person). Most dogs will want to do their normal doorbell behavior (bark, dash, growl, jump up for example).

As you begin to work with the door, you are going to need some way to keep your dog at the *go to*. If you are alone you can toss treats, but have a good aim in order to keep your dog on the *go to* (or to direct him back to it).

The Manners Minder (MM) is a remote controlled treat/food dispensing training tool that can be found online. It is a training device that will allow you to work with your dog if you are alone. You can use it in place of another person. If you have access to another person that person would remain near the *go to*, to reinforce your dog for being on it.

When adding the new context of the door be sure to start with the lowest distracting and least likely to trigger your dog scenario. Ringing the doorbell or knocking on the door may be too much to start out. I recommend that you first rattle the doorknob or make some door related noise, say nothing. If your dog leaves the *go to*, get him back on it (toss treat, use MM or have second person at the ready to remind). The goal of this part of the exercise is to get the dog on the *go to* when door action is happening.

Slowly add more activity at the door, such as opening it, saying hello or softly knocking, to name a few. Each time you will reinforce your dog for being on the *go to* in the correct position (lying down for example).

As time progresses you will begin to fade out your food reinforcement so your dog is going to the *go to* triggered by the EC (doorbell, knock or someone coming in) without the need for treats.

Be consistent with your training and the criteria you reinforce. Once you raise the criteria for reinforcement, stay at that level (don't reinforce sits and downs) so you do not confuse your dog. If you find you have raised your criteria too fast, go back one step briefly than try to move back up. Only raise your criteria when the dog is reliable at the current criteria. If you follow these steps you should be able to successfully set your dog up for success.

Loose lead – walking side by side
Your goal is to be able to walk with your dog on a loose leash alongside you. If you need to move between walking backwards and walking forward, do so. You want to make sure you prevent your dog from using pressure on the leash/collar.

This is not heeling. This is simply working on getting your dog to walk under control without applying pressure to the collar/leash.

Part of your goal for this week is to be very aware of when you are being moved by your dog. This literally means you do not allow your dog to direct your movement. Far too often I see a dog owner, arm outstretched, letting the dog navigate and actually pull the owner. It works because the dog puts a little pressure on and the dog owner moves forward; generally not realizing they are doing it. This teaches your dog to pull you around and becomes increasingly difficult to correct later.

I want you to consciously note what happens when your dog is on his leash with you. What do you do? How do you react to his pulling? When you are not walking; directing the movement, your dog should be standing, sitting or lying down quietly near you, not moving you from place to place.

Work on your hand position. When your leash is in your hand you should have your hand at your midsection; where your belt would be. If you need to hold onto your belt or the waist band of your pants, your hand/arm should never leave this position when operating your leash.

Pawsitively Unleashed!
Real life training for Real people.

Chapter Three Behaviors Log

Skill	Date	Date	Date	Date	Date	Date	Date	Date	Date	Date	Date
Down											
Extended Sit (down)											
Stand											
Position Changes											
Sit											
Down											
Stand											
Settle (Relax)											
Go To Place											
Loose Lead Walking											
Training Notes:											

How to use this log: Train using a set number of treats per session and mark down how many treats you actually use in a session. Example — session 1 dog received 5 treats for 5 correct responses

Chapter Four

Learning Concepts

Eliciting behavior
There are several ways to get your dog to perform a behavior; the following four techniques are among the most commonly used.

Luring: Think of the old donkey and carrot trick; this is luring. You literally take your treat (toy, hand, and so on) and use it to lead your dog into an exercise. It is a great way to get your dog going in the right direction. It is simple and basically anyone can lure a dog (a horse, a pig, a human, and so on) into a behavior.

Prompt (physical): Prompting is the use of physical means to manipulate your dog into a position. The most common prompt is to push your dog's butt into a sitting position. I do not recommend the use of prompts in dog training as they actually interfere with the learning process because they actually set off the opposition reflex in your dog (you push down, he pushes up).

Capture: Capturing a behavior is just that; catching your dog doing it with no prompt or cue from you. Capturing can be a great means of getting desired behaviors, but is not a fast means to do it as you actually have to catch the dog in the behavior. Capturing is good for trying to work on getting your dog to relax or settle as you would simply reinforce him when you find him doing so.

Shaping: I personally find shaping to be a lot of fun. Shaping helps your dog learn how to be creative and problem solve. It encourages and empowers him to think and use his brain.

Shaping is also referred to as free shaping. Shaping is about the use of approximations (baby steps toward the target behavior). You would use shaping for more complex behaviors and behavior chains (several behaviors to create one behavior). Teaching a dog to sit is a pretty simple behavior. Teaching your dog to flip a light switch would be a more complex behavior. You would use shaping by marking every small step behavior your dog does that will clearly (or not so clearly) lead the way to the target behavior. When shaping you must know your target behavior so you can create a training plan, which would include the approximations you think you will be working on. I say think, because you may have a plan and find your dog has a different one, but end up where you wanted to be just the same.

It is however, not the best method for all behaviors.

Release cues
It is important you use a verbal cue (or hand signal) to release your dog from a behavior exercise. By not doing so, you are allowing your dog to determine when he is done. While it may seem like no big deal, it is. Your dog needs to understand you are the one in control, by determining when an exercise is finished you are letting him know you are.

For those sneaky dogs that get up before you release, you can still work some magic. When you see he is about to break the exercise, tell him he is done. He then begins to associate the release cue with him finishing and you can back your way into the release by cue from you.

Training Exercises

Attention

Begin adding attention to other exercises, especially the loose lead-walking side by side exercise. The more you can keep your dog watching you, the more you have him ready to be responsive to you.

Reach for collar—"gotcha"

Many dogs have an aversion to having their collar grabbed. It typically means nothing good is coming (the end of play time, being kenneled, leaving the park and more canine sadness). It is a good idea to help your dog to see collar grabbing as a good thing. Simply grab the collar and treat. Keep your dog guessing when someplace like the dog park by doing some collar grabs with treats so he does not assume the grab and go scenario.

Appropriate meets and greets

Meet a friendly stranger: It is appropriate for your dog to sit politely when you encounter someone while out for a walk, as well as when someone comes through your door, if for no other reason than legal safety for you.

Practice in a low distraction area with someone familiar to the dog. As the person approaches have your dog sit quietly. The approaching person should turn and walk away if your dog breaks his sit. You will use the actual approach of the person as reinforcement (the person walking away is actually punishment if your dog truly wants to see him) for the dog remaining in his sit. The approaching person can either pet the dog or offer a treat, and must immediately ignore the dog and turn away if your dog moves out his sit without being released to do so.

Approaching another dog: When dogs approach one another it is even more important that they do so under control, especially when on lead. Leash tension is a major contributor to dog-to-dog aggression episodes. It can turn what could have been a neutral greeting into a nightmare in an instant. When dogs are on lead pulling toward one another it creates artificial antagonistic body posture, it also creates frustration and stress for the dog that is pulling, which in turn can create aggressive behavior toward the approaching dog (or other dogs over time).

When you are approaching another dog, whether you plan to let them meet or not, make sure your dog is on a loose lead and attentive as well as responsive to you. Do not allow your dog to pull you to the other dog. If your dog is pulling and out of control do not continue the approach. If the other dog is clearly pulling and not in control do not continue as approaching another dog should be done calmly, especially when on lead.

To practice this, begin by trying to find another dog you can use so you can set up the approaches in a meaningful and systematic manner. Begin with each dog on opposites side of the street (or some similar distance if not in town) walking from opposite directions so there is an approach and pass situation. If at this distance your dog (or the other dog) begins pulling and becomes reactive, stop, slowly back up as you talk to your to dog until you are far enough away your dog is again responsive. Mark and reinforce your dog for being attentive to you. Then turn to walk back again. You will repeat this back away behavior every time your dog shows signs of reactive versus responsive behavior. You want him to learn how to act. Do not punish or in any way give attention or reinforcement to the reactive behavior. Simply back away until you have responsive behavior.

As you are able to continue to move past the other walking dog with a controlled pooch of your own, begin to close the space between while still walking in opposite directions. Close the space slowly. Do not go from opposite sides of the street to the same sidewalk. Move one dog to the space between the sidewalk and road and repeat the above until your dog is able to notice the other dog and have no real reaction or will look at the other dog then look at you. Each step closer should be done slowly to prevent your dog from being put into a position that will make him want to react.

Your goal is to be able to walk on the same sidewalk and approach with a responsive and controlled dog. You can opt to let them sniff each other briefly and move on or simply walk past. Do not ever let them approach if either dog is reactive versus responsive.

You can further work with walking in parallel by first walking in follow the leader fashion. Have the least reactive dog in front and keep a safe distance. Slowly allow the dog at the back the opportunity to catch up and even quickly sniff the lead dog before backing off again. Remember, your dog cannot be pulling you, he must be under control before he is allowed access to the other dog. As you are able to have longer close proximity time, you can begin to walk up alongside the other dog. Keep a good eye on body posture and leash tension (any tension means back off or stop and move again as your dog is getting near his threshold). You want to keep the reactive switch in an off position.

Back away — reorient
Begin with your dog standing next to you on leash, simply make a weight shift and back up a few steps. Do not jerk or pull on the lead, just let the natural consequence of your backward motion do its trick. Your dog should turn and re-orient to you (mark, reinforce, repeat).

When your dog is good at reorienting to you up the ante and let him walk about while on lead before you take a step backwards. Your goal is for your dog to notice you have moved backwards and reorient to you.

The next step will be to move to a more distracting area and repeat those first two steps. You should also begin to work this exercise off lead in your original low distraction area.

Throughout do not encourage your dog to come to you, just let him make the choice to reorient on his own. This will allow him to learn what you want in a more meaningful way.

Reorient in this case means he moves with you and faces you.

Loose lead walking — close proximity
Play the catch me game with your dog whenever possible. To play put your dog's leash on then let it drag (or use a tab). Begin to move in a large circle encouraging your dog to follow you — so be fun. When your dog actually gets alongside you reinforce him with a jackpot of some sort (treat, favorite toy, game he likes, and so on), repeat. Each time you play the game raise your criteria by making a smaller circle, or expecting him to be alongside you for longer periods, to get there quicker etc.

You do not need to tell him anything special as you only want to reinforce his being alongside you. You can begin to raise the criterion to having him in the actual heel position (his shoulder in line with your pant seam).

Recall — toy
As a changeup to the chase recall, grab a toy your dog loves and run with it as you tease your dog. Your dog should be happy to see this chase/play and join in. Before he catches you, turn to face him with your legs shoulder width apart and toss the toy between your legs so your dog has to run through you to get the toy. Your goal is to get your dog heading straight on to you with enthusiasm.

You will work up to running, teasing, turning with legs together, use the toy to lure a sit, wait 5 seconds, collar grab, release with a big dash of toy retrieve.

Pawsitively Unleashed!
Real life training for Real people.

Chapter Four Behaviors Log

Skill	Date	Date	Date	Date	Date	Date	Date	Date	Date	Date
Attention										
Reach for Collar										
Appropriate Meets/Greets										
Friendly Stranger										
Another Dog										
Back Away - Reorient										
Loose Lead Walking										
Recall-Toy										
Training Notes:										

How to use this log: Train using a set number of treats per session and mark down how many treats you actually use in a session. Example — session 1 dog received 5 treats for 5 correct responses

Chapter Five

Learning Concepts

Body blocking

Body blocking is a handy skill you can use to prevent your dog from accessing something or to keep him out of trouble. It can involve your entire body or simply a part (for example, your leg).

Body blocking is not used as a form of punishment (or reinforcement), it is strictly a management tool. As a management tool it should be used temporarily, not in place of training for appropriate behavior.

Body blocking can be used to teach your dog behaviors such as 'leave it' since it works on the concepts of pressure and release (of pressure).

Body blocking is not giving your dog a knee in the chest to prevent jumping up, but it is you leaning forward to prevent it.

Body blocking works because dogs respond to pressure. When working stock with my dogs, applying pressure with my position allows me to move the dogs where I want them, as they move to release the pressure.

Be sure not to body block in a situation that could cause you harm from a dog bite.

Time outs

A time out for your dog is the same as it would be for a human child. You remove the dog for a short period of time. A time out should never exceed 1-3 minutes. Beyond that time your dog has no clue why he is there and the lesson is lost.

Time outs are a form of negative punishment. You are removing something in order to end a behavior you find inappropriate. When your dog is getting crazy, or mouthy or simply out of control, giving him a time out will give him a second to settle.

When using a time out, you must be consistent. This means you must always use the time out if you tell your dog you are going to do so. I tell my dog "time out" when he is having impulse control issues with his house mates. I use a "two strikes and you are out" approach. He has learned at the first time out to change his behavior and the need for an actual time out is almost gone.

Like body blocking, time outs are a management tool to be used in coordination with your behavior modification and/or training program.

Pre-heeling - walking in the box

This dog is working within the box; his shoulder is less than 1 foot from my leg (or pants seam). Photo © 2MC Design

Pre-heeling — walking in the box

Work on having your dog walk alongside you in an imaginary box of approximately 1 foot by 1 foot by 1 foot (one foot in front, behind or alongside you). Your dog should only receive reinforcement when walking in this box, with a loose leash.

Recall — be still and come

Work on doing a recall while you are stationery. You may need to start just a foot or less from your dog in a very low distraction area. Have your dog on leash with the leash on the floor and you standing on the very end of it. Say your dog's name and encourage him to move toward you using your verbal cue when he gets to you for the first 10 repetitions. Repeat this process at the same distance, but use your verbal cue when your dog is half way to you for the next 10 repetitions. Repeat this process at the same distance, but use your verbal cue when you call your dog to you. You can only use the verbal cue ONCE, if your dog does not come go back to the halfway point. Repeat the process from further away and start with your verbal cue, when your dog gets to you, then again using the verbal cue at the halfway point and again using the verbal cue to call your dog to you.

Sit (down) on cue — with distractions

It is time to get your dog to sit when you cue him to do so under a variety of distractions. Distractions can range from a person walking around to tossing a toy to tossing treats on the ground to other dogs playing and more. The sky is the limit with your distractions.

> A caution on distractions: start low and slow. Move toward higher distractions, as you want to set your dog up for success. Your distractions should not only vary in type but in location to help your dog begin to generalize that sit means sit anywhere he hears it.

Stays — close proximity

When you extended sit (down) is reliable, you are ready to begin stays. I always suggest you start with the position your dog is most likely to perform for any period of time. You will remain in close proximity to your dog and be very aware of your body, as you do not want to accidently set up a body cue you don't realize you have used.

Begin by putting your dog in the position of choice and mark/reinforce the position after 5 to 10 seconds and release. Continue to do this raising the duration criteria by 5 seconds each time until you can have your dog remain in this position for a minimum of 2 minutes. You are not using the verbal cue "stay" yet, just working on the duration of the sit (or down or stand).

When your dog will remain in this position for the minimum of 2 minutes, without moving or needed to be redirected you are ready to add the verbal cue "stay". Start again with your 5 to 10 second stay and work your way to a minimum of 2 minutes.

Practice this with all three positions (sit/down/stand) until your dog is able to do a stay for a minimum of 2 minutes in all 3 positions.

Check-in

Whenever possible work on getting your dog to simply check in with you. Every time your dog comes to you for any reason, say "Check-in" then praise, pet, treat, play or something your dog enjoys. You are trying to get your dog to understand check-in simply means they come over to you. It is not a recall. You can add a collar grab as well and the reinforcement for checking in is release and "Go play."

Be sure you start out in low distraction areas, like home. If you go to the dog park, you can work on this as well by taking some high value reinforcement. When you see your dog heading your way be ready and say "Check-in" when he gets to you. After awhile you can begin to say "Check-in" when he is on his way to you and progress to actually calling "Dog Check-in" when he is out of sight. Remember, when he is out of sight you must wait a bit to give him a chance to get to you.

You can also make this a default behavior by simply reinforcing your dog each and every time he comes to you. In this way you are encouraging your dog to come check-in with you from time to time on his own accord.

Stay — add distance

Once your dog has a solid stay, you are ready to move on. Make sure you have a good solid two minutes of duration first.

Depending on where your dog is sitting or doing a down (in front of you or alongside you), you will get your dog in a stay and move away one step. If your dog is next to you, step one footstep away with the leg that is furthest from your dog. If your dog is facing you take one step backwards.

You will want to step away a step or two at a time and reinforce your dog for remaining in a stay. The idea is to reinforce the stay as you move away, not to move away as far as you can right away.

When you are able to move about 5-6 feet away from your dog without him moving from the position you left him in, work on getting to the two minute duration again. You will need to go back to a few seconds and work your way toward the two minute mark, but will get to it quickly.

If your dog breaks the stay body block and/or lure him back into position, reinforce and release using your verbal cue. Move and start over, but go back to where you were last successful (5 feet away 45 seconds for example).

Heeling — precision

It is my believe that when training your dog you should train him to perfection. Train as if you are looking at winning the highest honors in an obedience trail and except nothing less than a picture perfect performance. My reason for this is simple. When we are in the training process we work hard and have expectations, when we slow down or stop training we get lax and slack off. If you train your dog to the level you can live with, your dog will get sloppy and revert back to where you started. If you train to perfection, your dog will get sloppy and end up with what you can live with.

Heeling is the precise placement of your dog's right shoulder in line with the seam of your left pant leg. I do not care which side your dog is on, just that his shoulder is in line with your seam.

You will only reinforce for that position and you will not move to do it. This means when your dog is where he should be he gets something when not, you do not lean, stretch or move around to get him the reinforcement, he gets nothing.

Do not worry about a verbal cue at this point as you want your dog to work on the behavior.

If you are still having trouble with your dog pulling on his lead, return to backing up and reinforcing your dog for following you on lead. (See **Chapter Two**, under *Loose lead walking* for more information.) Also work on standing still and clicking when your dog puts slack in the lead so he understands the goal is to have no pressure on his neck.

Chapter Five Behaviors Log

Skill	Date	Date	Date	Date	Date	Date	Date	Date	Date	Date
Pre-heeling										
Recall-Be Still										
Sit on Cue-Distractions										
Down on Cue-Distractions										
Stays-Close Proximity										
Check-In										
Stay-Add Distance										
Heeling - Precision										
Training Notes:										

How to use this log: Train using a set number of treats per session and mark down how many treats you actually use in a session. Example — session 1 dog received 5 treats for 5 correct responses

Chapter Six

Learning Concepts

Understanding target behaviors

Target behavior is the actual behavior you are working on teaching. It is important to understand exactly what the target behavior is. You should be able to describe it in order to achieve it.

When teaching your dog, define your target behavior. For more advanced skills, map out the steps you think you will need to get there. I say "think" because your dog may take you in a totally different direction but still get there.

An example of a target behavior would be "lie down on a mat with hip rolled." This is a much better description than be on the mat. It defines exactly what you will be teaching your dog. It adds consistency to the process as you now have an exact picture of what you are trying to achieve.

I suggest you work on using defined target behaviors whenever you are teaching your dog something beyond a basic sit. You will find your sessions to be more productive for both you and the dog.

Goal setting

Goal setting is another excellent concept in teaching (anything not just your dog). Goals fall in with realistic expectations. What is the ultimate goal of your training? Are you looking for the next obedience trial champion? Are you wanting a well-mannered family pet? Are you hoping to do therapy dog visits? Planning on playing in the agility arena? Is your dog destined to be working your livestock?

You may find as you train your goals begin to change, and that is ok. Knowing your goal allows you to set realistic expectations and will better aid in you in defining target behaviors.

Training Exercises

Recalls with distractions (toy, chase)

Begin to work on your recalls in increasingly distracting situations. Be sure to set your dog (and yourself) up for success. The goal is not to make it so distracting your dog blows you off; it is to make sure your dog understands to come to you in a variety of circumstances.

Use both the chase and toy recall exercises to get your dog coming in to you. When your dog gets to you, have him sit in front of you before you reinforce.

Once your dog is good at coming to you and sitting in front of you, reach down and grab his collar before reinforcing. This will help your dog learn to come to you, sit and have his collar grabbed as part of the entire behavior. In the future, you will be happy he does.

Touch-n-go game — impulse control

The goal is 60 to 0 in a flash. Use this fun and fast game. Get your dog all cranked up and ready to roll. When he is really ramped have him stop and offer a nose touch to your hand. The idea is get your dog to deal with calming quickly.

This game should be played in increasingly more distractive and crazy situations. Do not use a situation so crazy or distracting that you are unable to get your dog to touch.

To play the game, start by playing with a favorite toy. Do not toss the toy but rather tease and tug with it. Suddenly stop and say "touch" with your hand out. When your dog comes to touch, immediately say YES or click and begin to play again. No food is needed for this game as the reinforcement for stopping to touch is going back to play. Each time you call your dog out to touch slowly increase the amount of time between the touch and resuming play. Your goal is to get your dog to break from excitement and calm down for a period of time.

Four corners — position changes

This week work on walking your dog under control and at each stop you make have your dog perform the behaviors-sit, down, and stand. The goal is to work on your dog's understanding of the behaviors by doing them in groups.

> Be sure you do not ask for the behaviors in the same order each time or your dog will get wise and perform them before you ask. Also make sure your dog complies with the behavior you cue before you move to another (in other words do not cue sit, and reinforce a down).

T-shirt game — handling

Practice handling your dog all over and having him love you for it. T-shirt is optional. Using a shirt on your dog forces you to touch him all over. It is a weird and novel experience for him. It also makes a fun game. Put your dog in a shirt and reinforce. If your dog is not good at being handled, you will need to progress slowly. Hold a foot — reinforce. Touch an ear — reinforce. Shirt over head — reinforce.

Chapter Six Behaviors Log

Skill	Date	Date	Date	Date	Date	Date	Date	Date	Date	Date
Recalls with Distractions										
Touch-n-Go Game										
Four Corners										
T-Shirt Game										
Training Notes:										

How to use this log: Train using a set number of treats per session and mark down how many treats you actually use in a session. Example — session 1 dog received 5 treats for 5 correct responses

Chapter Seven

Last Minute Learning Concepts

Reinforcement vs. Reward
Many people confuse reward and reinforcement, understandably.

Rewards are offered as incentive to do something, or something given for performance of a worthy behavior.

In animal training, the most commonly used form of reinforcement is food, often confused with a reward for behavior.

Rewards are also considered bribes and thought to be something one must always have in order to gain the behavior. You only work because you get paid. If you stop getting paid, you will most likely leave your job.

Reinforcement is something that happens in direct relationship (timing) to a behavior that will increase the likelihood it will happen again. It can be contrived (a treat, toy, game) or a naturally occurring consequence either external or internal. Reinforcement is directly responsible for increasing the likelihood a behavior will be repeated.

Rewards are nice to get, but do not necessarily mean you will repeat a behavior, and in fact, may happen in a circumstance that has no need for behavior increase. Christmas bonuses can be looked at as a reward for being employed at just the right time. It does not mean you will still be there next Christmas.

Attention splitting
This is a great skill to develop and perfect. It is actually your skill.

Attention splitting is just as it sounds. You split your attention between your dog and the rest of your world.

The easiest way to get good at attention splitting is to work on your dog doing a "settle" while you are sitting and doing something (watching TV, playing on line, and so on). Your dog is to remain in that position so you need to keep track of the dog while you are doing something else.

Bite prevention
Every year preventable dog bites occur, simply because people do not act accordingly or do not supervise them when in the presence of children.

An estimated 4.7 million people are bitten each year by man's best friend, most of which are children, bitten by the family dog or a dog known to them.

Understanding what dogs are telling us and how to interact with them in a proper manner is essential in preventing bites. Learning how to act appropriately with all dogs, including the family dog, is also essential in preventing dog bites from occurring.

Dogs as a general rule DO NOT like to be hugged and held.

A dog's body language will tell you if he is uncomfortable, ignoring this can lead to a bite. Dogs who turn their head away with part of the white of the eye showing (whale eye or half moon eye) are showing signs of distress and could very well bite.

Another sign is a closed mouth and "hard stare." This is a dog making a decision. Comfortable dogs tend to have their mouths open, and are panting lightly.

Here are some rules to follow to prevent dog bites:

- Never pet a strange dog, without asking the owner first. Never pet a strange loose dog.

- Ask the owner to have their dog sit, if they are unable to do so, you should walk away.

- Do not run up to a strange dog (or your own), and do not scream and yell.

- Never put your face up to at dog's face; this can be seen as a direct threat and you risk being bitten in the face.

- Never allow children to play with the dog unsupervised, and never leave an infant in the room with a dog unsupervised.

- Do not allow children to pull on the family dog's ears, tail, fur, and so on, as another dog will not be so tolerant.

- Never punish a growl; it is the dog's way of telling you he is not comfortable. Punishing a growl will not change how the dog is feeling about a situation, but taking away his growl can lead to a bite.

- If a strange dog comes running up to you, Be a Tree. Stand still with your arms at your sides and hands in a fist, look down and avoid eye contact. Do not make any sound or move. If the dog begins to jump on you or should knock you down, curl up and be a rock, similar to a tornado drill pose you will get on your knees and bend your body so your head is on the floor and put your hands up over your neck, head to protect them.

- Do not bother a dog that is eating, especially if he growls, leans over this dish or offers any other threatening display.

- Socialize puppies with as many people and experiences as possible in a positive and non-threatening way. Attend a dog training class with your dog to learn how to properly teach him how to act appropriately in your home.

For more information on dog bite prevention visit www.doggonesafe.com.

Canine communication

Dogs do not communicate like people communicate, yet have developed the skills to understand humans despite the fact that people are generally clueless as to what a dog is trying to communicate.

Dogs are constantly communicating; people are constantly ignoring it (unintentionally).

People are constantly communicating incorrectly in dog terms, but dogs "listen" and learn and interrupt to make it meaningful.

Poor communication between canines and humans lends itself to behavior issues, aggression and misunderstandings.

Growling: Growling is a dog's first line of defense. Dogs growl to increase distance. A growl signifies discomfort or unease in a dog. Growling should never be punished or reprimanded as it is important communication; punishing a growl will lead to the next step distance increasing behavior, which is a bite.

Displacement: When feeling anxious, unsure or uncomfortable, dogs exhibit displacement behaviors; they can include tongue flicking, yawning out of context, shaking off as if wet, genital licking, sniffing the ground, looking away, submissive grins to name but a few. These behaviors help a dog redirect and regroup and also lets others (actually "listening") that the dog means no harm, is not confrontational and is safe.

Piloerection: When dogs become aroused the hair along their back goes up. It is not always a sign of aggression. You must look at the whole picture (dog's tail carriage, ear set, mouth) to determine what it means.

Family Companion Dog - Overall Progress Log

Skill	Date	Date	Date	Date	Date	Date	Date	Date	Date
Attention									
Sit on Verbal Cue									
Default Behaviors									
Introducing the Marker									
Leave it									
Approximation #1									
Approximation #2									
Approximation #3									
Loose Lead Walking									
Recalls									
Name Response									
Handling									
Down									
Extended Sit (down)									
Stand									
Position Changes									
Settle (Relax)									
Go To Place									
Reach for Collar									
Appropriate Meets/Greets									
Back Away									
Check -In									
Training Games									

How to use this log: Train using a set number of treats per session and mark down how many treats you actually use in a session. Example — session 1 dog received 5 treats for 5 correct responses

Appendix: Odds N Ends and Extras

The following handouts are included as a quick reference.

www.pawsitivelyunleashed.com

How Dogs Learn

2011 © Renea L. Dahms DipCBST, RMT, CTDI

Like any other living being, dogs learn by trial and error, reinforcement and punishment. This is the basis for learning and behavior. If a behavior pays off, it will be repeated. In other words it has been reinforced. If a behavior nets a negative reaction it is more likely to diminish or go away entirely and it can be considered punished. If a behavior that was previously being reinforced no longer receives reinforcement, but is not punished either, it is being put on extinction and will most likely die a natural death.

Reinforcement and punishment are not as simple as cookies or spankings and the definition is the effect on the behavior itself. Simply put if a consequence increases the likelihood the behavior will repeat, the behavior has been reinforced and if the consequence increases the likelihood the behavior will decrease or go away, the behavior has been punished.

Confusion in training comes about with the addition of the terms positive and negative. In learning and behavior positive means the addition of something, not an emotional state and conversely negative means something is taken away, again not an emotional reaction.

Reinforcement is said to be positive or negative with either increasing the likelihood of the behavior repeating or getting stronger. The quick and easily understood example of positive reinforcement is the dog sits, he gets a treat. Assuming it was a treat the dog found valuable and wants, he will sit again in hopes of gaining another. Negative reinforcement would be the removal of a stimulus that still increases the likelihood the behavior occurs. Traditional choke collar training and today's high fashion e-collar (shock collar) training are based on negative reinforcement. When heeling, if the dog lags behind or forges ahead, a quick snap, choke correction is applied; when the dog returns to heel position the correction is removed. The dog learns to get back to heel position upon hearing the rattle of the chain collar or feeling the shock to avoid the choke or make the shock go away. Eventually the dog learns to remain in the correct position to completely avoid the choke or shock. The method is still considered reinforcement as it increased the likelihood the behavior (in this example, heeling) occurs.

Punishment too is positive or negative, meaning something is added or removed to decrease likelihood of a behavior being performed again. Kneeing a dog in the chest when jumping up, in which the dog stops jumping up would be positive punishment. Bark collars and underground fences are also positive punishment, as the dog receives something he wishes to avoid, so drops (or suppresses) the behavior to avoid the stimulus. Negative punishment would be a time out. The dog is running amuck or jumping up, the owner turns her back or leaves the room or the dog is removed from play due to biting or excessive behaviors. Something is removed the dog would like to have (owner's attention or play) so the behaviors decrease in intensity or go away all together to avoid this loss in the future. The behaviors were punished.

When teaching your dog what is appropriate, the best bet is to use positive reinforcement, as the goal is increasing desired behaviors. To avoid fear, pain and loss of trust or eroded bond, positive reinforcement works best. Punishment does serve its purpose, but should be used in extreme moderation and when employed must be done correctly (more on this later). When teaching young puppies positive reinforcement should be the only consideration for increasing desired behaviors, and the use of punishment should be limited to removal or time outs.

Behavior Markers

2011 © Renea L. Dahms DipCBST, RMT, CTDI

Animal training has relied on the use of behavior markers over time, but it was slow to make its way to the dog training world, for reasons totally unknown. Dolphins, Orca's and other mammals performing at Sea World and other ocean parks have been taught to perform natural behaviors, on cue and out of context with the use of a behavior marker and some food reward to not only reinforce the desired behavior, but to create behavior chains (complex sets of behaviors).

The most commonly known behavior marker in the dog training world is the clicker, a small plastic box with a metal tab that makes a click sound when pressed. Clickers themselves have become so popular they have new shapes, sounds and are marketed heavily. Like any tool, they must be understood and used correctly to work.

A clicker is also known as a conditioned reinforcer (it has also been known as a secondary reinforcer-as it is secondary to, say food, the primary reinforcer). The sound of the conditioned reinforcer lets the dog know a primary reinforcer is on the way.

A behavior marker can also be verbal, as in "good dog" or "yes". A clicker, bell, whistle or similar audible device makes a better behavior marker, because it is quicker, consistent in sound and never emotional, not to mention it is not the same background noise a dog hears day after day after day.

To be used properly the behavior marker must first be paired with primary reinforcement. This can typically be done in a few quick click-treat sessions. The idea is for the dog to understand first the sound means a treat is coming (or whatever you primary is), this is best done by doing a click-immediate treat to create the association. Next an easy behavior the dog already performs should be cued, with a click immediately upon success of the behavior, followed by a treat. This makes a new association for the dog, correct behavior gets this sound, which means a treat, which means do more of this behavior.

The correct use of a clicker is for the acquisition stage of teaching a new behavior or working on creating fluency of behavior to add a cue. Once the behavior is well established there is no more need for the clicker on that particular behavior. This is one area where clickers are most often incorrectly used.

The entire purpose of the behavior marker is to quickly and accurately mark a desired behavior with the goal of increasing the likelihood the behavior continues. It is a simple tool, but timing is important when using it, as the correct behavior must be marked in order for the dog to make the connection to the desired behavior.

Whenever using the behavior marker, a treat (or the primary) must follow every time or the meaning of the marker can become diminished.

It's All Just Sounds to Them

2011 © Renea L. Dahms Dip CBST, RMT, CTDI

Dogs are born with a complete communication system of their own, and not one part of it involves human verbal language (or human body language for that matter). Dogs do not understand words period. Dogs do understand the associations of words to behaviors, once the association has been made, either through formal training or trial and error (lack of actual training).

To dogs words are simply sounds. It is the responsibility of the owner to teach the dog exactly what meaning each sound has, and the appropriate response to it. In other words, when one says "sit" the dog puts his butt on the ground.

Words cannot hold dual meanings, so similar or same words should not be used for different behaviors. Think of the word 'down'. It is often used to get a dog to lie down, but then used to get the dog stop jumping up. Most often the dog complies with neither behavior, as how could he be expected to know which meaning it is?

For words to work as behavior cues (commands), they must first be given meaning, than used consistently. Do not ask a dog to sit, than reinforce a down. Do not expect to just say something and expect the dog to "just know" what it means or refers to. Children are given months and years to know or understand a word's meaning, yet it is expected the dog know it on first exposure, what sense does that make?

To make the word-behavior association, the dog must first understand the behavior and perform it with some fluency (will do it 8 out of 10 times), before a word can be tossed at it. Waiting for a dog to offer or perform the behavior, then adding the verbal cue makes the association go faster, and avoids the "multiple cue syndrome", where the owner says "Sit sit sit sit sit sit sit siiiiittttt" while the dog stands there looking around. It also allows the dog the ability to concentrate on what behavior is wanted without trying to sort out the barrage of sounds humans make.

When teaching a dog to perform any skill from very basic manners to advanced competitive sports, it is important to have a game plan of both the verbal cues (words) to be used and the exact behavior expected to go with it. This small amount of pre-planning will make everyone's life easier and training go faster. Be sure to stick to the plan, do not change verbal cues or use more than one for the same behavior, it will only confuse the dog and muddy the waters of the teaching sessions. Consistency and more consistency is a key component to the teaching process, and the ability to make the correct verbal cue-behavior association.

Pick words that are easy to remember, easy to say and have some meaning similar to the behavior (in human terms). While saying "rice pudding" to get a dog to do a down, may make for a fun parlor trick, it is not easy to remember and makes no sense in relation the behavior, so no one else is likely to use the verbal cue, causing confusion and frustration for the dog.

Once the dog has been allowed to make the verbal cue-behavior association in a systematic way, the cued behavior should become more and more reliable with repetition.

Capturing, Luring, Prompting & Shaping

2011 © Renea L. Dahms DipCBST, RMT, CTDI

Dog training is really the art of behavior manipulation. The goal is to get the dog to perform a certain behavior upon hearing or seeing a cue (command) in a specific manner, which can vary based on the person asking, the context and the exact situation or circumstance.

There are several ways to manipulate behavior and they include capturing, shaping, luring and prompting. Any method can be used on its own or in combination with another and there is debate over which ones are truly best.

So what exactly are they? I will explain them for you.

Capturing is simply catching your dog in the act of doing something you like and reinforcing it. Much like finding your kid doing the dishes without being asked, your dog will perform desirable behaviors all on his own. We all know that dogs can and do sit, lie down, not move (stay) and so much more, what we typically fail to recognize is the golden opportunity for reinforcement they offer. Capturing is simple to do; unfortunately most people are not "ready" to do so. When your wild and crazy dog finally does a nice lie down (out of sheer exhaustion or boredom, or why ever he does) tell him "Good Dog" in a calm tone and pet him. The whole idea behind capturing is to actually reinforce a behavior while it is happening. It can also be used in a more formal training set up, if you are willing to wait it out (attention is a good learning exercise for capturing).

Luring is as it sounds, you use something (treat, toy, movement) to lure your dog into a behavior or position. A commonly used lure is to take a treat back and over your dog's head, luring him into a sitting position. Many behaviors can be lured, and it is (or was) the staple of reward based training classes.

Prompting involves some use of physically putting the dog in a position. More traditional methods of training relied on this. An example would be the use of pushing a dog's hindquarters down to get him to perform the sit. I am not a huge fan of prompting, and feel many dogs taught in this manner have come to see the prompt as the cue and only perform when prompted to do so.

Shaping is similar to capturing in that you are working at getting a behavior from your dog without lures or prompts (or minimal lures), but what is reinforced are approximations of the behavior. This means not waiting for the exact behavior you want, but something that looks close or behaviors that would be small steps toward the behavior. Shaping is a fun way to train, it encourages your dog to think, problem-solve and be creative, it also really works well on building a bond. My favorite example of behavior shaping is one I use in my classes. I extend my hand out to the person before me. The person typically will reach out and shake my hand (even if with an amount of uncertainty), which I will reinforce. I will again extend my hand, a wee bit higher with the same hand shake result (click treat). I keep up this hand shake behavior at a higher and higher level until I am forced to stand on a chair, which forces the person to jump CLICK TREAT! I was shaping the jump behavior, so used other behaviors to get us there. Picture the jump as the top rung of our behavior ladder, the handshakes were rungs along the way.

The Attention Exercise

2011 © Renea L. Dahms DipCBST, RMT, CTDI

As with people, if your dog is not paying attention to you, it is difficult to communicate with him. The first exercise you will want to work on is teaching your dog to pay attention to you, or "watch you". For some dogs this can be direct eye contact, for other dogs it will simply mean looking in your direction, as direct eye contact can be intimidating (it is confrontational canine communication).

Attention is easiest taught by luring and/or capturing the behavior. It is best taught as a default behavior, or one that is cued by distraction versus one put on a verbal cue.

To begin luring for attention, simply start working in a relatively low distraction area, use a high value treat and let your dog know you have it. Move the high value treat from your dog's nose toward your face in such a manner the dog follows it with his face/eyes and click treat when he looks at your face (or directly into your eyes). Repeat this procedure several times. Do not say anything (a yes or good dog is fine), just work on reinforcing the behavior.

To capture the behavior, you can start by clicking and reinforcing any behavior that is close or a move toward attention. This can include the dog actually looking toward you, looking away from something of interest (head turn away from distraction), or something similar in nature. You will find you will begin to do a combination of lure and capture, with more lure in the beginning and more capture as the dog begins to understand looking at you is a huge benefit.

Once your dog is doing this with some consistency, you can begin to add small distractions, work in different locations and help the dog generalize the behavior. The idea is to work the dog toward more and more distraction to gain or keep his attention.

A word in adding cues. You can begin to add a verbal cue "watch" or something you will remember when the dog looks at you…"Watch"-click-treat. Using a verbal cue will remind your dog what you want if he does not use distraction as a cue to look to you. You can also put the behavior on cue, by the very situations. In other words when working with more distractions, if you simply reinforce the behavior of looking away from the distraction, then looking to you during distraction you can help the dog learn distraction = look at owner = something good. When this happens you will find your dog more inclined to look at you and less worried about what has him distracted in the first place.

Leash Handling 101

2011 © Renea L. Dahms DipCBST, RMT, CTDI

Leash handling is a learned skill. Proper leash handling lends itself to loose leash work from your dog.

The purpose of your leash is to protect your dog; it is not a steering wheel or a means to control your dog. The leash is simply to make sure your dog is not able to run off, be hit by a car or be involved in any other incidents.

Begin leash work without your dog attached so you can get proficient at it.

Put your thumb through the handle loop and form a fist with the loop in your hand. (Do not put your entire hand through, using your wrist. If your dog should quickly jerk, you can easily break your wrist and still lose your dog.)

Hold your hand at your mid-section to keep a good center of gravity and to prevent your dog from pulling your arm forward. I also suggest you work on standing in your best football stance, feet shoulder width apart and knees slightly bent.

Have another human around to grab the leash and tug on it. Your job is to remain standing with your leash in your hand, hand at your mid-section.

Dogs are typically given mixed messages with a leash. They lunge, pull and/or tug, jerking the human end of the equation, causing your arm to fly out; after a minute to regroup you pull your arm back in. This basically says "YES PULL" and "Get Back Here" in the same sentence. The goal is to prevent your dog from pulling your arm out.

Now add your clicker and some treats to the exercise. Again have your human leash tugger pull and tug your leash, when they stop doing so CLICK and hand them a treat (candy would be good). This is a great way to practice without having the stress of your dog.

When you begin working with your actual dog, be sure to start in the house or yard.

Hold your leash as described above, have treats ready and when your dog allows any slack click/treat. Slowly add more distraction to this exercise.

Loose Lead Walking-the Pre-Heeling Behavior

© 2010 Renea L. Dahms, DipCBST, RMT, CTDI

Before you can begin teaching the fine art of "heeling" your dog must understand how to walk with a loose leash. The length of the leash is not relevant as your dog must understand to walk with slack in all situations.

To start your dog working on leash with you, attach your leash and hold on to the end and let your dog have the slack or most of it. Do not hold the leash tight removing any slack as you are only teaching your dog to operate without slack and at the end of a tight leash with a lot of pressure on the throat. (The dog will walk at the end of a lead 1' or 100' with this method.) Get a favorite toy or treat and begin to walk backwards as you call the dog's name. Every time the dog gets to you give him the treat or a quick play with the toy and keep moving backwards. You are reinforcing the dog moving with you on a slack or loose lead this way. Walking backwards works well as dogs like to follow or chase things and they are more likely to walk toward you (since you are facing them).

If your dog rushes past you or does not follow try being more interesting by adding interesting sounds, running backwards, jumping up and down etc. and reinforce him for being near you. The goal is to get your dog to walk in the same direction you are without pulling and applying pressure from his collar.

Once the dog is following you reliably you want to reinforce him for being alongside you, so you will continue to walk backwards but instead of reinforcing for getting to you, you will turn and reinforce while the dog is alongside you. The goal is to keep the dog walking on a loose lead with you, but reinforce for being in the correct place. You will immediately turn back and keep walking backwards then turning to reinforce.

After some reliable repetitions you can begin walking forward with your dog. You only reinforce when the dog is near enough to get the treat from you. DO NOT reinforce by leaning to the dog, the dog must get to the correct position himself.

Remember that loose lead walking is NOT heeling. It is simply walking on the leash with slack and no pulling, lunging etc. Heeling can only be taught once the dog is reliable at loose leash walking, otherwise you are asking too much at one time. There is really no verbal cue in this stage of teaching your d (but terms such as "Easy" or "Walk Nice" can be used). You should encourage and talk to your dog though to keep him interested and engaged. I also suggest you start in a low distraction area to start, such as your own home. You can attach the leash and let it drag as you lead the dog around. Make it fun, make a game of it, the more fun it is the more likely the dog is to want to keep playing.

Reliable Recalls

© 2011 Renea L. Dahms DipCBST, RMT, CTDI

One extremely important behavior all dogs should perform and perform well is a recall. A recall is, as the name implies, the dog returning to the person upon a cue to do so.

The association you want to make with the verbal cue is the dog is near you. The traditional method was to say come and expect your dog to run to you across the yard. The main problem with that is the behavior that occurs around the cue is running, not necessarily running to you. Teaching your dog to associate the cue with being near you makes it more likely your dog will "get it".

The best way to start out teaching a recall is to simply praise and reinforce your dog for being near you. The idea is to create the association that good things happen by you. The fastest way to ensure your dog does not come to you is to make being near you negative, especially if he does show up after you call him. This means you should not behave in a manner that makes your dog uncertain or afraid to be near you.

To begin working on a formal recall, pick a quiet low distraction area and say your dog's name and run backwards. Do not say come or here or any other recall type word, just the dog's name and run backwards. When he gets to you IMMEDIATELY reinforce and say "here" or "come" or whatever your recall verbal cue will be. Continue with this game of running backwards, reinforcing and using your verbal cue.

As your dog begins to understand this game, say his name before he is to you and as he is running toward you. You want to make sure he will actually get to you at this stage and you will want to remain in a lower distraction area.

If the option is there, add a second (or third) person to the game and begin taking turns saying the dogs name, running backwards and reinforcing him for getting there. Try to keep who calls random so your dog does not get the rhythm of the game and just run back and forth without being called. Be sure to use the verbal cue, at first when he arrives, than as he is running.

To increase the difficulty, begin working on discrimination between hearing his name and actually being called. As a rule of thumb, the name is used to gain your dog's attention and have him ready for a cue (information). This can be especially important if as you are about to call your dog you note something, such as a car driving by or backing out, that could be an issue if your dog comes charging to you. Have your additional person hold the your dog (a long line is a good plan here) and say his name, but do not call him. Be sure your assistant does not let him go until you say your recall cue. Again the idea is for him to look to you upon hearing his name, yet wait to see what you want. Call him again this time with the recall cue and reinforce. This becomes the new game, but again be random with the recall cue to name only ratio.

As your dog gets better and better at the recall, start adding more and more distraction and working in places other than home, be sure he cannot take off or become injured where you are working.

If you continue to work in this systematic approach your dog will understand the meaning behind the recall cue, quickly and reliably. Do not practice it in a situation where your dog won't be successful, have a backup plan for those times in early training where things may go wrong.

Door Dashing Be Gone
& other threshold nightmares
© 2011 Renea L. Dahms DipCBST, RMT, CTDI

Door dashing can be the rush to say hello, or the mad dash for any open doorway, especially if escape to the outdoors is the goal. With a little bit of preemptive strategy you can prevent your dog from ever developing a strong behavior history with this annoying and dangerous behavior.

This behavior encompasses more than simply rushing the front door and can become an issue with any threshold (car door, house doors, crate doors, etc) and in some cases may require a bit of training time at each threshold. There are also different motivations for each dash, for instance going for a walk may be so highly exciting that your dog literally drags you out upon being leased, release from a crate is highly rewarding (especially if your dog is not a crate fanatic) and can cause craziness, and in multi-dog homes the release of one dog from a crate may send the other dog into a frenzy of crazy behavior. At any rate these environmental changes happen and your dog must learn to act appropriately when they do.

Impulse control goes a long way in curbing the door dashing dog. A great exercise for this is the automatic watch your handler. The ideal picture here is using the Attention Exercise, where you teach the dog to look to you when things get crazy. When using it with thresholds the idea is your dog goes out the door, then turns to look at you, preferably in a sit instead of racing out the door, dislocating your shoulder. A waist leash is a great tool here as it gives you a good center of gravity and keeps your dog from really moving you much if at all, and sends a clear message that pulling works no more.

To begin working on the default threshold move, you need a threshold. A door leading to somewhere your dog wants to be is a great place, but could be too great to start out. Pick a door to a more boring place, like to the bathroom or some neutral area. Simply open the door and allow the dog to walk through it, you stand at or just in the threshold without passing through the door way waiting there until the dog looks back at you and immediately reinforce. When you first start this exercise, you can say the dog's name, but nothing else until he looks to you. In most cases he will look to you quickly, as you are not moving with him and this is probably not normal. No matter why he looks back, reinforce it as it the behavior you want.

When you find your dog picking up the look back from the doorway, you can begin to ask for more. This can be looking back at you from a closer spot (especially if he is at the end of his lead now), or a sit or down. At this point your dog is used to being reinforced for looking back, but may offer another behavior if you do nothing when he does look back. What begins to happen here is the dog knows some behavior interaction with the door equals a good thing, and to date that is looking. If he is still away from you, he may move closer to you, or offer a sit (assuming he does a reliable sit now). At any rate, wait him out and see what happens, if he offers you a behavior you like or is close to what you actually want reinforce, then work at getting more and more until you get the exact behavior you were hoping for (i.e. dog goes through door, turns toward you and sits).

Now that you are getting what you wanted in a boring area, move to a better door and start over. You will note this goes much faster. You can also look at using going out that door as reinforcement, instead of treats, after all reinforcement is reinforcement and does not have to be food. With time you will have a dog that no longer makes a mad dash to and/or through the front door when leaving.

Appropriate meetings and greetings at the door are an absolute possible dream, but are handled in a different manner. If your dog is currently rushing the door, a very quick band-aid fix is to have some treats at your door that you can ask your guests to toss on the floor away from them and the door. The idea is to get the dog looking down and moving away. This is just what you do while actually trying to work on a nice mannerly sit away from the door, so do not rely on it as your finished behavior, but more as your go to back up plan so your dog does not have the ability to keep practicing the inappropriate behavior.

A great way to get a mannerly sit (or down) is to teach your dog to "Go To" (a mat, bed, area rug etc) that is placed away from the door, yet in a place where he can actually see the door. Being able to see what is happening is actually important in this exercise or it becomes too difficult for the dog to remain sitting out of the loop. If done in a systematic manner which allows your dog to be successful at each step, you can actually have your dog cued to go sit (or down) in the designated spot upon the ringing of the doorbell, or knock on the door.

The very first step is to teach your dog to interact with the "go to" of your choosing. Simply reinforce him for any interaction, a foot on the "go to", sniffing etc., continue to do so until the dog understands the "go to" is the key to his reinforcement. Continue to reinforce him for interacting with the "go to", but pick on behavior (foot on for example).

Once your dog is reliably performing the initial interaction raise the criterion. If your dog was putting one foot on the "go to", now expect him to put all four feet on it for example and continue to reinforce only this behavior. Again you will raise the criterion, normally dogs will sit when all else fails and reinforce this. You can raise your criterion to a down (preferred).

Be sure you are standing near the "go to" so your dog is most likely to interact with it.

Now that your dog is performing the target behavior on the "go to", step one or two steps away and start over. Most likely your dog will sit on it, or just near it. You may have to walk over toward it so your dog is on the "go to" and back up before you click. The idea is to reinforce being on the "go to" while you are not right next to it, but do not go too far.

Continue this until you can go to your door with the dog on the "go to" and send your dog to the "go to".

Now begin to add the door. Begin by rattling the door, wait ½ second for your dog to "go to" then cue the behavior-click/treat (toss it). You will play with the door, then open the door, have someone outside open and peek in, door knock, doorbell and any other door behavior common in your home. Each time give your dog ½ a second to "go to" before you use a verbal cue. You ideally want your dog to simply be cued by the door to "go to", but in a pinch you can send him.

Sample Training Logs

Chapter One Behaviors Log

Skill	Date	Date	Date	Date	Date	Date	Date	Date	Date	Date
Attention										
Sit on Verbal Cue										
Default Behavior										
Introduce Marker										
Training Notes:										

How to use this log: Train using a set number of treats per session and mark down how many treats you actually use in a session. Example — session 1 dog received 5 treats for 5 correct responses

Pawsitively Unleashed!
Real life training for Real people.

Chapter Two Behaviors Log

Skill	Date	Date	Date	Date	Date	Date	Date	Date	Date	Date
Leave It										
Approximation #1										
Approximation #2										
Approximation #3										
Loose Lead Walking										
Recall-Chase										
Chase										
Toy Chase										
Name Response										
Handling										
Training Notes:										

How to use this log: Train using a set number of treats per session and mark down how many treats you actually use in a session. Example — session 1 dog received 5 treats for 5 correct responses

Real life training for Real people.

Chapter Three Behaviors Log

Skill	Date	Date	Date	Date	Date	Date	Date	Date	Date	Date
Down										
Extended Sit (down)										
Stand										
Position Changes										
Sit										
Down										
Stand										
Settle (Relax)										
Go To Place										
Loose Lead Walking										
Training Notes:										

How to use this log: Train using a set number of treats per session and mark down how many treats you actually use in a session. Example — session 1 dog received 5 treats for 5 correct responses

Real life training for Real people.

Chapter Four Behaviors Log

Skill	Date	Date	Date	Date	Date	Date	Date	Date	Date	Date
Attention										
Reach for Collar										
Appropriate Meets/Greets										
Friendly Stranger										
Another Dog										
Back Away - Reorient										
Loose Lead Walking										
Recall-Toy										
Training Notes:										

How to use this log: Train using a set number of treats per session and mark down how many treats you actually use in a session. Example — session 1 dog received 5 treats for 5 correct responses

Chapter Five Behaviors Log

Skill	Date	Date	Date	Date	Date	Date	Date	Date	Date	Date
Pre-heeling										
Recall-Be Still										
Sit on Cue-Distractions										
Down on Cue-Distractions										
Stays-Close Proximity										
Check-In										
Stay-Add Distance										
Heeling - Precision										
Training Notes:										

How to use this log: Train using a set number of treats per session and mark down how many treats you actually use in a session. Example — session 1 dog received 5 treats for 5 correct responses

Pawsitively Unleashed!
Real life training for Real people.

Chapter Six Behaviors Log

Skill	Date	Date	Date	Date	Date	Date	Date	Date	Date	Date
Recalls with Distractions										
Touch-n-Go Game										
Four Corners										
T-Shirt Game										
Training Notes:										

How to use this log: Train using a set number of treats per session and mark down how many treats you actually use in a session. Example — session 1 dog received 5 treats for 5 correct responses

Family Companion Dog - Overall Progress Log

Skill	Date	Date	Date	Date	Date	Date	Date	Date	Date	Date
Attention										
Sit on Verbal Cue										
Default Behaviors										
Introducing the Marker										
Leave it										
Approximation #1										
Approximation #2										
Approximation #3										
Loose Lead Walking										
Recalls										
Name Response										
Handling										
Down										
Extended Sit (down)										
Stand										
Position Changes										
Settle (Relax)										
Go To Place										
Reach for Collar										
Appropriate Meets/Greets										
Back Away										
Check -In										
Training Games										

How to use this log: Train using a set number of treats per session and mark down how many treats you actually use in a session. Example — session 1 dog received 5 treats for 5 correct responses